Ta Chuan

Ta Chuan

The Great Treatise

Stephen Karcher, PhD

ST MARTIN'S PRESS ⚹ NEW YORK

First published in 2000 by St. Martin's Press
175 Fifth Avenue
New York, NY 10010

Created and Produced by

Carroll & Brown Limited
20 Lonsdale Road
London NW6 6RD

Senior Managing Editor
Christina Rodenbeck

Deputy Art Director
Tracy Timson

Editor
Dawn Henderson

Designer
Gail Jones

Library of Congress Cataloging-in-Publication Data
in process.

ISBN 0-312-26428-3

Printed in Italy by L.E.G.O.

First edition

10 9 8 7 6 5 4 3 2

Through Change,

a Realizing Person knows the subtle and the obvious,

the supple and the strong.

So act with Change and be a model for the myriad people.

Contents

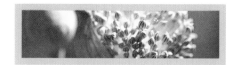

SECRETIVE SAGES
According to Taoist legend,
the Seven Sages hid in
a bamboo grove, taking
refuge from the horrors
of the Warring States
(c. 500–221 BCE).

spirit world. It tells you how to use these things to effect a profound transformation in your life.

    Ta Chuan maintains that the symbols of this old divination system "contain" or "participate in" or "match" the fundamental processes that create the world around and within us. It says that sages and spirit-mediums "set out" Change and that what it calls the "Sage-Mind" is contained within it. For the *Ta Chuan* Masters, Change is a spiritual presence and a teacher without peer. By using Change you experience a fundamental connection to the on-going process of the real, a transformation of character and a liberation from compulsion and fear.

The Book of Change

Ta Chuan speaks much about Change. *Ta Chuan* uses this word to mean several things, but the most important is the divination book and technique called *Chou I*, the *Change of Chou*, or, later, *I Ching*, the *Classic of Change*. Throughout this book, I will simply call it Change, the way it is referred to in *Ta Chuan*. This is a sophisticated collection of divinatory symbols with specific techniques to consult and interpret them.

In traditional cultures, the power of a symbol was valued highly. Divination revealed the will of the Gods, the great forces that control and shape the world. Divination also carried a culture's myths and stories through its system of symbols, and gave people access to these myths. It was a place where the individual and the great archetypal images could interact. Divinatory practices permeated traditional societies, producing medicines, reading omens and sky signs, judging quarrels, determining propitious moments and relaying messages from non-human powers.

BEGINNINGS

What we now know as the *I Ching* or *Classic of Change* began as a loose collection of omens and symbols, a shared divinatory language that goes back to at least 5000 BCE. The words and symbols of this language probably originated with the *wu* or spirit-mediums, who could speak with the voice of the spirits. The first written record of this language occurs on the oracle bones, a vast library of pyromantic divination as practiced by the Shang Dynasty kings (*c.*1600–1100 BCE). The Shang kings used this Fire and Bone oracle frequently, particularly in their relations with the ancestors on whom their power depended.

THE NEW ORACLE

The symbols of the divinatory language were first assembled in the Chou Dynasty (*c.*1100–500 BCE). The relations between the Shang and the Chou are a very important Chinese myth. According to this myth, the virtuous Chou rulers overthrew the decadent Shang rulers and re-established a long-lost Golden Age in China. Their reign became a model for all kings to come. They claimed they were able to do this because they had been given the Mandate of Heaven (*t'ien ming*), taken away from the Shang because of their evil and irresponsible behavior. A very important part of the mandate was a new oracle, a much more effective version of the language and practice called Change. It was the *Chou I* or *I Book of the Kings of Chou*, the first form of the *I Ching*.

This *Chou I* was revolutionary in many ways. It used 64 six-line figures to organize and display the symbols of the divinatory language. To access these figures, Chou diviners originated a method of dividing and counting a set of 50 yarrow stalks to produce at random the numbers associated with the lines. This was explosive. It meant that instead of going into full trance, or setting up the very complicated ritual apparatus for the Fire and Bone oracle, you could know the way the spirits were moving through a simple 30-minute ritual. This made *Chou I* a very important strategic tool.

By about 600 BCE, *Chou I* had gone through several revisions and had become quite sophisticated. It developed the capacity to assimilate and use most of the other systems it came in contact with. The people who used it, however, were changing. It was no longer the exclusive privilege of the Chou kings. Professional diviners moved among the centers of power and culture. The text was available to anyone with the ability to read. The symbols became an integral part of culture, immediately recognizable even outside the context of a divination.

THE WARRING STATES

Over the next 300 years, China fell apart. The Warring States period (c.500–221 BCE) was a time of constant civil war, radical social change, destabilization and great suffering. This fragmentation gave rise to the fundamental books of Chinese culture, among them the Confucian classics *Lun yü* and *Meng tz'u*; the Taoist masterworks *Lao-tz'u* and *Chuang-tz'u*; the utilitarian philosophy of the Legalists *(Han Fei-tz'u)*; the universal love and logical arguments of *Mo-tz'u*; and the extreme individualism of *Yang Chu*.

The Warring States period is considered the golden age of Chinese philosophy, the most creative period in the culture. But this burst of creative activity occurred against a darkening background of social breakdown and civil war. Iron weapons developed, forced conscription was used to raise armies and scholars became a floating class, seeking employment at the courts of the various unscrupulous warring princes. Here is a description of the end of this period, taken from a later Taoist text, the *Huai Nan tz'u*:

"In later generations, the [warring] states set up clan differences … raising armies and attacking one another. When they laid siege to cities they slaughtered mercilessly, overthrowing the nobles and threatening the innocent. They dug up burial mounds and scattered the bones of the dead … Out of a hundred who advanced, only one would return.

In these circumstances, the able-bodied and light-footed were made armored soldiers [fighting] a thousand *li* away, while family elders and feeble ones remained at home, sad and sick at heart. Menials and stable grooms pushed carts and distributed rations along endless roads in biting frost and snow, and their coarse felt clothing did not cover them. Others, exhausted, their carts falling to pieces and road mud reaching up to their knees, pulled one another along highways. They struggled with their heads on the road, fell prostrate on the crossbar of their wagons and died.

What the expression "annex the states and appropriate the land" meant was several hundred thousand dead bodies and smashed chariots ... The world finally reached a point where people used human skulls as headrests, ate human flesh, pickled human livers, drank human blood, and relished these more than the flesh of grass and grain-fed animals."

The great questions for all were "How can we save ourselves and our culture? What is the Way (Tao)? How was it lost?".

The spiritual use of Change grew out of this breakdown that engaged thinkers, diviners, magicians and poets. It affirmed a radical faith in the experience of a helping spirit (shen) and developed specific techniques to contact it. The Masters who developed the Way of Change introduced something that was quite new— divination as a spiritual practice. But they described it as the re-invention of something very old. This is the central idea behind *Ta Chuan*, The Great Treatise.

THE NEW EMPIRE

The chaos in China came to an end in a devastating total war. Soon after, the short lived Empire of Chin gave way to the stability of the Han Dynasty (226 BCE–220 CE). After three hundred years of war and chaos, China was at peace at last. One of the tasks undertaken by the many bureaucrats and scholars of the new Han government was to reform the written language in order to establish, among other things classics or *ching*. These works, it was felt, represented the wisdom of the ancient peoples and contained a very powerful magic. The first among these classics was the *I Ching* or *Classic of Change*.

SYMBOLS OF CHANGE
This ornate bronze disk shows the eight trigrams with their corresponding Chinese characters and the yin and yang or t'ai chi symbol in the center.

The scholars, however, did more than establish the text. They collected the oral "traditions" or *chuan* that had grown up during the Warring States period, transcribed them and added them to the basic divinatory text. With these additions, called the Ten Wings (*Shih I*), *Chou I*, the divination text of the Chou kings, became *I Ching*, inspiring a tradition of philosophical and mystical speculations.

FIGURES OF CHANGE

Ta Chuan discusses the divinatory symbols or Figures of *The Book of Change*. Literally, a symbol is a combination of lines, diagrams, words, signs and their associations. *The Book of Change* is made up of 64 of these—the real divinatory material, the book's symbolic reality.

At the time of the *Ta Chuan*, a Figure consisted of a six-line diagram (*gua*), thought to be made up of two three-line diagrams (also called gua). There were words, phrases and divinatory signs attached to the hexagram as a whole, and other words, phrases and signs attached to each one of its six lines. The gua are made up of combinations of two different kinds of lines, one whole or continuous, the other broken or opened, representing the two primal powers that form the world. There are eight possible three-line diagrams (the Eight Diagrams or *Pa Gua*), and 64 possible six-line diagrams, the basis for the 64 Divinatory Figures of *The Book of Change*. The Diviner would determine the type and order of the lines in the hexagram using a "chance" procedure. This is held to have been the throwing of yarrow stalks. A group of words, phrases and signs called the Image or *T'uan* is "attached" to each diagram. The first word of the group is used as the Name of the Figure. Other words are "attached" to each of the lines. *Ta Chuan* says these words and phrases were perceived by Sage People and spirit-mediums. They can have many, sometimes contradictory, meanings and can act as any part of speech, in any person or tense.

EIGHT TRIGRAMS AND THEIR ATTRIBUTES			
TRIGRAM	IMAGE	ACTION	SYMBOL
☰	**Force** *Ch'ien*	Persisting	*Heaven*
☷	**Field** *K'un*	Yielding	*Earth*
☳	**Shake** *Chen*	Stirring-up	*Thunder*
☵	**Gorge** *K'an*	Venturing/Falling	*Stream*
☶	**Bound** *Ken*	Stopping	*Mountain*
☴	**Penetrating** *Sun*	Entering	*Wood Wind*
☲	**Radiance** *Li*	Congregating	*Fire Brightness*
☱	**Open** *Tui*	Stimulating	*Marsh*

Here is an example of a Figure in modern translation, along with a paragraph that summarizes traditional and modern commentary on it.

24 Returning

upper/outer trigram   6th line

5th line (center)

threshold _____ 4th line

3rd line

lower/inner trigram   2nd line (center)

1st line

Return: go back, turn back, come back; return to the starting point; resurgence, renaissance, rebirth; renew, renovate, restore; again, anew; the beginning of a new time.

Image

Returning gives you Success.

Things go out and in, come without affliction.

Your partner comes without fault.

Your Tao reverses and returns you to the Way.

Returning comes on the seventh day.

It is advantageous to have a direction to go.

Commentary: Rebirth and returning energy after a difficult time. Go back to meet it and begin anew. This will bring success. Return to the source, the original feeling and purity. Let things go out and come in without difficulty. People suggest profitable projects. Joining with them is not a mistake. Your way is reversing direction and will return to you on the seventh day, the completion of this period of time. You can begin again. Having a plan or direction brings profit and insight. Be open to new ideas. Turn to meet what is coming. Returning to the Way is the source of virtue and power. Guard yourself and let the energy return. Stir your energies up and work with the movement. Allow things to emerge. Heaven is moving in these events. By returning to the Way, you will see the heart of Heaven and Earth.

Later, other texts were associated with the basic Image. Here are various divinatory texts and perspectives from the Ten Wings.

Sequence

You can't completely use things up.
When you exhaust stripping above, it reverses itself below.
Accepting this lets you use the energy of Returning.

Definition

Returning means reversing.

Symbol

Thunder is located in the center of the Earth. Returning.
The Early Kings barred the passages at winter solstice.
Sojourning Merchants did not move at winter solstice.
The Crown Prince did not inspect things at winter solstice.

DIVINATORY SIGNS AND TRIGRAMS

Another kind of character appears in these texts, which *Ta Chuan* calls a divinatory sign—a specific guide to action. The two basic signs are "the Way is open" (*chi*) and "the Way is closed" (*hsiung*). Others are "success," "advantageous," "without fault" and "shame and confusion."

In the six-line diagram, we see two three-line figures or trigrams, one above, one below. In this case they are Shake (Chen) and Field, (K'un). These have many associations in divination.

☰☰ **Shake,** Chen, is the Thunder spirit who bursts forth from the Earth to arouse, excite and stimulate things. This spirit stirs things up and brings them out of hiding. It can give you the strength to undertake difficult things. Its symbol is thunder; its action to rouse and excite. It is made up of one stirring strong line below two supple lines. In the family it is the first son.

☷ **Field,** K'un, is the womb that gives birth to all things. It nourishes everything without judging. It can give you the power to make thoughts and actions visible. Its symbol is Earth; its action is to yield, to serve and bring forth. It is made up of only supple lines. In the family it is the mother.

A diviner can use these and many other associations to weave a web of meaning. As the two trigrams interact, they suggest a dynamic between inner and outer worlds.

Inner and Outer: Shake and Field.

Rousing new energy germinates inside and opens a new field of activity

Each line in a figure also has a specific text attached to it. The line texts are called *yao*, a mysterious word that probably means "calling out." The yao texts are triggered when a line "transforms," changes its shape and becomes its opposite. This is said to mirror the transformations or changes of form we face in life, among them the experience of death. An unchanging line is called "continuing" and does not trigger a text.

The yao lines are the most important and most "telling" texts in determining what specific action should be taken in a given situation. They are usually the center of attention in a divination. In the samples we have of old divinations it is usually the *yao* line that is spoken of, in a direct poetic fashion. If we had a "calling" line in the fourth place of our example, for instance, it would bring up the following text:

Six at Fourth

The center is moving, return alone.

Commentary: The center of things is moving. Sense this and move with it, even though you must go alone. Do not be sorry. You are returning to the Way.

Taken together, the words, diagrams and lines allow you to intuitively perceive one of the most characteristic and mysterious things in *The Book of Change*, the symbol (hsiang). *Ta Chuan* insists on the power of the symbols. Virtually equivalent to the Tao or Way, they can only be seen with the imagination. They are the way in which we can penetrate the mystery of transformation and connect with the bright spirits. The key to entering the symbolic realm is to "turn and roll" the words in your heart. If you do this, the symbols will spontaneously appear. This can literally change the way you perceive reality and invite greater powers. Here are some of the possible meanings of the term translated as symbol.

Symbol, hsiang: image, to resemble; invested with the intrinsic power to connect the visible and invisible; magic spell; omen, portent; shape, figure, form, diagram, pattern, model; create an image, act, play, imitate; write, writing; law, rule; stars and constellations.

The Golden Age

The Golden Age is one of the most powerful myths in Chinese culture. This was the time when time began, the source of all that is valuable and precious. It was a time before history. The Golden Age was peopled by ancient sages, beings of superlative insight and wisdom. Because they lived at the beginning of time, they could see what would unfold in the future. The ancient sages were beings of deep, all-encompassing compassion. They cared for all, not just those around them. Their thought lives on in our hearts, where time is only relative. They are with us in our imagination still.

This is not just a primitivist fantasy. The sages represent a way that people can live in connection with gods and spirits. They are symbols of a deep layer of human imagination, a repository of spiritual wisdom and experience. Most Chinese recognized that when they talked about the sages and the Golden Age they were talking about something both symbolic and utterly real. Traditionally, whenever someone created something particularly profound he would realize "it was written by the ancient sages."

FLOWING FROM THE SOURCE

Humans have put considerable effort into creating symbols to explain time's shape. One paradigm is the symbol of "origin" or source, often imagined as a spring. This origin or source is a beginning of time. It can occur anytime or anywhere. The oldest layer of Change uses it as a fundamental divinatory sign: *Yuan*.

Yuan means what is fundamental. It can be translated as origin, spring (both the season and the source of flowing water), and first or primary. It means great, excellent, potent. It connects the vernal season, the East and sunrise and contains the actions to issue forth, to begin, to appear. It signifies the first sign of day, the first power in the cosmos, the headwaters of a river, the source of our thoughts, the source of authority, the eldest, the head, the chief, the original.

This is one of the oldest ideas of time. The river and the infinitely varied movements of water offer a model: sources, wild rapids, still pools, underground streams, falling rain, the circling sea, the blood that surges through the veins in our bodies, mist returning to the sky. This is the world of the shamans and spirit-mediums, potent individuals whose contact with the unpredictable spirit world helped the people around them survive and move with the changes in the time.

THE ETERNAL ROUND

The beginning of agriculture gives us another fundamental kind of time, a "sacred round" that repeats itself indefinitely. It is based on the regularity and stability needed to grow cereal crops and grows out of a careful observation of what recurs in the sky through the seasons. The fertile earth in all its moods becomes an important deity. Its different faces are the stages in an eternally recurring cycle.

The cycle of crops is repeated in the cycle of life. Just as a day goes through certain recognizable changes, so, too, does a human life. The most frequently used metaphor for cyclic time is the Four Seasons. They epitomize all processes of growth, decay and renewal.

THE AXIAL AGE

In many ways, time and change are synonymous. Change can only happen in time, and time without change simply disappears. *Ta Chuan* insists that Change contains or "participates in" all kinds of change and time. It contains the eternal flow, the alternation of the

雲歸巫女粧猶潤
楊妃睡未醒

FRAGRANT SYMBOL

A traditional symbol of perfection and purity, the lotus features often in Asian art. This delicate Chinese watercolour dates from the 19th century.

seasons, the dance of sun and moon, the transformation from life to death. But Change or *I* is more than that. The word I, the name of the book, above all means trouble—unpredictable, destabilizing change; change that dissolves structures and destroys cycles.

Historically, the equivalent to this quality of I is a Time of Troubles, what one philosopher called an "axial age." An axial age is violent and disorganized. The stable institutions of a culture break down. Central control ceases to function. But at the same time, this is a powerfully creative period. All the paradigms, the potential models for new ways of thinking are on display. It is much like a personal breakdown, when the old personality doesn't work any more and a new one must, eventually, be constructed. It is during these times, both personal and public, that we can reach back to the ancient sources.

DRAGON HOLES, SYMBOLS, AND THE SOURCE

Somewhere around 700 BCE, there was a great meeting of diviners, magicians, historians and sages in Northern China. The Golden Age of the Chou Dynasty was moving rapidly toward another Time of Troubles. As a last attempt to correct the time, this group of elite "technicians of the sacred" decided to collect, organize, edit and set forth for general use the sacred divinatory language and practice called Change which might open a hole or window in time that looked to both past and future. The diviners and magicians assembled at the edge of their world were desperately hoping they could create one of these windows.

Here we see another important kind of time. Though the flow of time may appear fixed or implacable, there are unique moments called "dragon holes," usually associated with breakdown and flux, when we can intervene and change the flow. We do this through symbols. Symbols are the very stuff of time. They can change its flow and direction. Through the divinatory symbols, we can reach back to a mythic time when humans lived happily and freely with spirits and allow that energy to flow into the present. This is the Golden Age. It is the source of time and the mystery of the Way.

Confucius and Confucianism

Several different schools of thought grew out of the fragmentation of traditional values during the Warring States period. All of them, in one way or another, were concerned with putting an end to the civil and emotional disorder by returning to the Tao or Way. However, each school had a very different idea of what that Way might be. The two most important schools, the Taoists and the Confucians, formed an opposition that shaped the rest of Chinese history. They became the two poles of the traditional culture's soul.

CONFUCIUS

Confucius or Kung-fu-t'zu (551–479 BCE) was the first of China's moral philosophers. He had little impact in his own day, but the philosophy that was developed out of his thought went on to dominate political, social and family life.

As soon as they acquired power, Confucians prohibited or re-interpreted all other forms of thought. The first of these re-interpretations was Change, which became a Confucian text. Their official interpretation of the words and images was made part of the Imperial Civil Service examinations. Investigating the deeper meaning of the text and discovering new moral axioms was one of the primary things a Confucian bureaucrat would do in retirement.

The official Confucian re-interpretation of Change began in the early Han period (150 BCE). In the late Han Dynasty, Tung Chung Shu, a prominent Confucian official, designed a cosmology and a method of analysis to contain and fix the multiplicity of Change, using yin-yang and Five-Process theory. About 250 CE Wang Pi re-arranged the words of *The Book of Change* and wrote the first complete interpretation of the images and lines based on Confucian morality. The first of the Five Confucian Classics, it was commented on and pondered for 1700 years.

What did Confucians believe? What made them so eager to suppress all other meanings but their own? The answer lies partly in the personality and the position of Confucius. Profoundly conservative, he came from an aristocratic family that dwindled, becoming poor and unimportant. He lived his life in the middle of social change and a great fragmentation of values, all of which he deeply despised. He felt that something great—a source of ultimate value—was being lost in this change. This was the world of his hero, the Duke of Chou.

Confucius deeply idealized the feudal aristocracy of the Eastern Chou (*c.*1100–771 BCE). For him, the rulers were sages whose moral perfection connected them to Heaven. The Chou kings had received Heaven's mandate. The power of Heaven flowed through them and let them clarify and fix eternally the proper relations between people of all ranks, divinely sanctioned in ritual and propriety (*li*). These rites and rituals (*li*) defined behavior on every possible occasion. As long as people kept to them strictly, the favor of Heaven would flow.

SCHOOL OF THOUGHT *Confucius taught his students how to achieve moral and social perfection in an effort to recapture the Golden Age.*

GOING TO SCHOOL WITH THE MASTER

Confucianism is above all a moral and a social philosophy. Austere and conscious of duty, it is the authoritarian father in the Chinese soul. Confucius insisted on evaluating all things through their moral worth. His work was education and it was open to all. Its goal was the creation of "gentlemen" who could advise people in power and rule a state as the Duke of Chou might rule it. Later Confucian thinkers described the goal of this education as the transformation of the personal mind *(jen hsin)* into the Tao mind *(tao hsin).*

The basic task is *cheng*, rectification. The world is in great disorder. To help, we must start by re-organizing our own characters and rectifying our own conduct. When we set foot wholeheartedly on this road of self-rectification, we join the ranks of the *Chün Tz'u*— the new nobility, a new class based on moral perfection. The Chün Tz'u "takes humanity *(jen)* as his burden." He is the moral vanguard of society, dedicated to bringing back the Golden Age.

The Chün Tz'u's first step is *hsiao*, filial piety. This is the cornerstone of moral excellence and the model for all relationships. It consists in embodying the family in your heart as the model of all human relations, including responsibility to the dead. The family is the source of life, and the model for the human family is the cosmos. As Heaven and Earth have a strict order and a hierarchical relation, so must the members of a family: the wife is subject to the husband, children are subject to parents, and young siblings are subject to older. You must internalize the rites, responsibilities and ritual behaviors that govern these relations.

The overall goal in the education of a Chün Tz'u is *jen*: humanness, benevolence or fellow feeling. It is expressed through virtues such as liberality, diligence, truthfulness, steadiness, earnestness and the willingness to reflect on things at hand. Jen has two sides: loyalty *(chung)* to your own moral nature, and treating others as you treat yourself *(shu).* The man of jen is a man of virtue. The price he pays is a constant watchfulness over his thoughts and feelings.

THE IMPORTANCE OF LI

The single most characteristic word in a Confucian education, however, is li: rites, ritual behavior, codes of behavior and propriety. Confucius was an expert on ritual. He felt that the rites—the way that people behaved in the time of the Duke of Chou—must be scrupulously and meticulously re-enacted. Our behavior and our most intimate feelings should be in accord with these gifts from the Golden Age. "To repress yourself and return to the rites is jen," Confucius said. Another saying refers to his punctiliousness: "If the mat is not straight, the Master will not sit on it."

This need to force the present into the ideal of the past is the source of the Confucian's need to eliminate anything that he cannot fit into his own moral pattern. Confucianism has often been called a rational or humanist philosophy, but at base it is as magical as the ways of thought it condemns as superstitious. Even in its most refined manifestations, the core of Confucian philosophy is the need to bring back the Golden Age through a transformation of language and behavior. But magical thinking is really not the question. The real question is "Which age is golden?"

Taoism and the Tao

If Confucianism is the harsh, stern father of the Chinese world, Taoism is its accepting and yielding mother. Its mood is joyful and irreverent. It is open to the occult and metaphysical side of experience that Confucians keep at a distance. Taoist ritual permeates popular culture. It is part of a religious tradition that includes trance, spirit mediums and spirit journeys, exorcism and psychic transformation.

The philosophical side of Taoism rests on two books, the *Lao-tz'u* or *Tao Te Ching* and the *Chuang-tz'u*, both composed in the Warring States period. Each contains deliberate and often hilarious attacks on Confucian moralism and heroic egotism. But Taoism is more than a reaction. It is a spiritual affirmation of chaos, spontaneous creativity and the central importance of "doing nothing" *(wu wei)*.

The Lao-tz'u or Tao Te Ching

The *Lao-tz'u*, the oldest Taoist classic, is a book for rulers. It suggests how a ruler can rule through Tao and not-acting (wu wei) rather than violence and exploitation. When the ruler loves quietude and acts only by not-acting, the *Lao-tz'u* tells us, his people will spontaneously follow the straight path and prosper. His genuine simplicity makes them passionless and still. He does not disturb their peace with analysis, speeches about virtue or ambition. He knows that when you use intellect, the great lies begin; when you disturb families, "dutiful sons" arise; when you have confused everything with your silly plans, "loyal subjects" appear. All these things have no Tao. By trying to do any of them, you end up with the opposite.

Taoism condemned the ideals of Confucian moralism—its virtue, its laws, its love of form and its hierarchical view of the family. Most of all it despised giving things names (*ming*) that subsume the thing in a category. By naming what you desire and taking the name for the reality, you split the opposites and call up your nemesis. Indeed, it is by striving to "do good" that we bring evil into the world.

So what can we do? Taoism extols the way of "nature," unanalyzed, uncivilized and unassertive. The way to act in the world is to take on the woman's role—weak, flexible and clinging. There are many images for this: water, the uncarved block, child, female, mother, valley spirit, dark door, empty vessel. It is the womb of creation. The Man of Tao opens this space within himself. Through it he returns to the source of all things. Tao, the mysterious highest good, manifests itself in his spontaneous, non-aggressive behavior.

CHUANG-TZ'U

Chuang-tz'u is the first Chinese text to present a philosophy of private life, a way of wisdom for the individual. Every educated man's ambition in Warring States China was to become counselor to a prince. *Chuang-tz'u* depicts these politicians as well-fed, decorated oxen being led to slaughter while he, a happy piglet or an old turtle, blissfully plays in the mud. Everything in *Chuang-tz'u* is designed to teach you the relativity of values and help you dis-identify with conventional ideas. It is also the first appearance of a special kind of spiritual being, the *Hsien* or Immortals, who have so successfully freed themselves from mundane existence that they have left the turbulent world. Their effortless existence, free movement and natural spontaneity became an image of Taoist perfection.

WOMAN OF THE TAO
Taoism has many aspects—male and female, human and immortal. Its maternal, patient, and slightly sardonic face is captured in this Ch'in Dynasty (c. 221–207 BCE) figure of a seated woman (opposite).

Taoist Education

The basic principle of Taoist education is emptiness. The Man of Tao creates a void or empty space in his heart by freeing himself from compulsive naming, greedy passions, and collective values. This opens the spontaneous action of the Way. Things begin to happen of their own accord. You do not will them.

Return is another basic principle. Let everything return to its starting point. Return is the movement of the Way. The Man of Tao, having created a void within himself, can return to nature's source and wander freely, watching the coming and going of the Myriad Beings. He sees the Way shaping the universe out of chaos, while yin and yang transform it. As he grasps this, his whole identity becomes fluid. He becomes like a spirit, a shen. Tao practitioners who empty themselves and dis-identify with collective values are said to acquire enormous *te*, power and virtue. Te helps you be who you were really meant to be. It gives you the power to realize Tao in action.

The central practice, however, is wu wei, not-acting. Wu wei is an idea, a meditation technique and a way of being in the world all at the same time. The Man of Tao never acts, but there is nothing left undone. Not-acting is not inaction. It is ceasing to act through the ego and the will, and beginning to act through the spirit (shen) and the Tao. There is no true achievement without this practice. Using force will eventually turn into the opposite of what you intend. Disaster and failure await.

The Sages and the Golden Age

Confucians saw the Bronze Age warrior culture of the early Chou (*c.*1100–771 BCE) and its feudal hierarchy as a Golden Age. Taoists idealized Neolithic farming villages and their spontaneous rhythms, where there were no books and no written language to trap people's minds, no "cunning contrivances" to excite their lust and no measures, virtues and laws to make them scoundrels and thieves. People didn't "fight to the death over profit."

All trouble arises when we lose sight of the Whole, when we split something off and call it "good" or "right." So, says *Chuang-tz'u*, offer no resistance to your opponent, discard your knowledge, throw away good and evil, don't meditate, don't cogitate, follow no Tao and you will attain it.

The ideal of the sage *(sheng)*, the goal of most Chinese philosophies, is also different for Taoists and Confucians. The Confucian sage is a culture hero, a ruler of antiquity who taught people the rites and rituals. The Taoist sage is more elusive—an internal quality *(nei sheng)* that moves in and out of the world of time and space. He embraces the Way, a fertile chaos full of the original energy *(yüan ch'i)*. He has a powerful, beneficial influence on his surroundings, the charismatic power *(te)* of the Way.

An Encounter

Let us imagine a brief dialogue between a Confucian and an old style Taoist on the subject of *The Book of Change*. Let's begin with the Confucian. This is the fellow responsible for turning *The Book of Change* into an officially enshrined text. Although it is anachronistic, I want to introduce Chu Hsi (1130–1200), the key figure in Neo-Confucian thought, to represent the Confucians. Chu Hsi represents a way of mind, systematic moral values and duty to parents, elders and the state. He wrote a moral interpretation of each sentence of *The Book of Change*, he popularized divination to insure that people used it as often as possible, and he articulated an attitude toward *The Book of Change* that lasted well into the twentieth century.

Chu Hsi sees *The Book of Change* as entirely moral and political. He finds talk of spirits and souls completely beside the point. Each person, he tells us, has two kinds of mind, a "person-mind" *(jen hsin)* and a "Tao-mind" *(tao-hsin)*. Most people remain stuck in the person-mind, frozen in selfish desire. That is why the Tao is lost, times are bad, and the state is in such trouble.

"It is our social responsibility to activate and cling to the tao-mind, through submitting each action to Change in its moral interpretation," Chu Hsi proclaims. "Our interpretation of Change is a direct copy of the mind of Heaven and Earth. Using it will rectify and clarify your filthy person-mind. This moral transformation is the necessary foundation for the regeneration of the individual and the state. It has nothing to do with souls and spirits; it has everything to do with correct moral principles. You will learn these in our Change."

Chu Hsi's principle is the proper hierarchical relation between things. This is what he wrote into *The Book of Change*. This hierarchical relation reflects the will of Heaven. Paradise is the time when these relationships were clear, the time of the early sage-kings who civilized the people by introducing feudal order.

Sitting directly across from Chu Hsi, making rude noises at the most serious parts of his diatribe, is the Taoist. His is a way of the heart and individual experience. Where the Confucian is dressed in ceremonial robes and wears an elaborate badge of office, this fellow is a wanderer, monk or recluse. He has no official "face." His wit mocks and deconstructs the Confucian's seriousness. For him, paradise is the "chaos-time" before the culture heroes who Chu Hsi so esteems messed everything up with "self-righteous meddling."

Here is a famous text from the *Tao Te Ching* that we can imagine him proclaiming with glee:

> *It is when Tao is lost, that your so-called virtue arises.*
> *It is when virtue is lost, that your so-called benevolence arises.*
> *It is when benevolence is lost, that your so-called righteousness arises.*
> *It is when righteousness is lost, that your so-called doctrine*
>   *of propriety arises.*
> *Now this propriety of yours*
> *is nothing but the empty husk of loyalty and faithfulness.*
> *It is the beginning of all confusion and doubt.*

The word "propriety" *(li)* is a key Confucian term of highest value, so this diatribe is quite insulting. It undermines the meanings of all of the Confucian's key words.

This sort of dialogue went on in China for many years. The Confucian erects a value system and the Taoist mockingly undermines it. It could even happen within the same person. An official out of office, unjustly dismissed, would find himself reading *Chuang-tz'u* and laughing at all hollow official honors. A year later, however, he would be called back to office and once again become the most diligent of Confucians.

Wu, Shen, and the Symbol

The most common Chinese word for a visionary who helps society is *wu*. This word is often translated as "shaman," but a wu's practice only distantly resembles that of the shaman, who, for the most part, are today located in Siberia and travel in "alternative realities" as part of their religious practice.

Siberian shamans are very aggressive. In trance, but in full possession of his faculties, a shaman may climb the World Tree to the Heaven of the Ancestors or descend to an Underworld in search of lost or trapped souls. He engages in battle with other shamans and persuades or battles with spirit beings. A shaman is "called" to his vocation. He undergoes a difficult and painful initiation, a ritual death and rebirth. Shamanism is characteristic of nomadic groups, without agriculture or a fixed living place.

In contrast, the wu is much closer to a spirit-medium. Through natural ability, training and ritual preparation, the wu can "call down" the bright spirits. The spirits inhabit the bodies of the wu and speak through them. This "possession" develops into a long-term, intimate relation between spirit and medium.

The most vivid example we have of such a practice today is *vaudun* in Haiti, where a participant is "chosen" by a spirit and becomes that spirit's "horse." Possession is total; the "horse's" voice, behavior and movement change completely. He retains no memory of the possession afterward—others must tell him what happened and what the spirit said.

Other traditions of mediumship, however, including those practiced today in the Far East, show that with training, the medium develops the ability to "split" awareness and remain conscious of the visit of the spirit. The medium can move in and out of the spirit's voice and conduct a dialogue with it. It is this awareness that characterizes the earliest descriptions we have of the experiences of the wu. The medium remains conscious of the spirit. Deep affection and joy characterize the encounter.

Visitors in the Spirit World

The *wu* were said to be possessed by *shen*, by divinity or spirituality, which descended into them in consequence of their powerful imagination. Often they would "drum and dance" to induce the descent. It was the presence of a wu at family meals shared with the ancestors—the oldest and most fundamental form of Chinese spirituality—that induced the spirits to "come down." At ancestral sacrifices the *shi* or "Embodier of the Dead" would go into trance and become the deceased ancestor, inviting him to eat and drink through his person. The spirit's presence at the ritual meal caused felicity and blessing to descend on all. These meals were the most common religious ritual in early China. Most members of the elite classes would have had the experience of becoming a *shi* and inviting the spirit to make use of their bodies.

In early times, wu were an important part of government and culture, acting like sages through the presence and words of their spirit or shen. As well as being the focal point of sacrificial ritual, the wu performed divination and exorcism. The spiritual imagination of the wu was perceived to be of great value and they were recognized as the model of sages.

According to early sources, *wu* were people whose souls were reverent, upright and inward. They had the wisdom to interpret signs in both Heaven and Earth. Their sanctity could illuminate what was distant and let it speak with clarity. Their great intelligence illuminated the good spirits; their discrimination understood the bad spirits. It was for this reason that the light of the gods *(shen ming)* descended into them.

But the Confucians ridiculed the *wu* and eventually outlawed them. Chu Hsi (see page 37), who articulated the practices of Neo-Confucianism in the Southern Sung Dynasty (1127–1279 CE), was vociferous against them.

THE GHOSTS AND SPIRITS

The wu dealt with what were called *kuei shen* or ghosts and spirits. These represented the basic kinds of non-human beings that share the world with us. Their interaction gives us a profound insight into how spiritual divination works.

Kuei and shen are opposites, as yin and yang are opposites. They represent kinds of experience that connect directly to the way Chinese see the psyche. In Chinese thought, we have two kinds of souls, *hun* or volatile soul and *p'o* or dense soul. The hun is thought, spirit in the blood, intensity and insight. It rises at death to eventually become shen. The p'o is the life of the body and its basic processes. At death it goes into the earth and the tomb. It is the p'o as an ancestor that is offered sacrifices. If it is angered, it may return as a kuei.

Shen is a "bright spirit" that is very potent and very mobile. In the oldest thought, shen existed outside the individual. Sages and mediums would go through elaborate ceremonies to induce the shen to take up residence in their bodies. Through this "in-dwelling" they acquired a helping-spirit. The shen confer intensity, clarity and depth on the soul. They make the oracle work and are "conjured" by its numbers.

OPPOSITE ELEMENTS
Yin is a thunderous cloud and yang, the fiery sun— like kuei and shen— on this page from a 19th-century Taoist weather manual.

Kuei are quite different. Kuei do not like to move. They are dark, earth-bound spirits. They become malevolent ghosts through anger, insult and injury, or hunger. Kuei easily poison a person or a situation, spreading psychic contagion. They cause a paralysis of the personality that leads to literal or spiritual death. They represent a deep negativity, pain and anger with which we must come to grips.

Divination seeks to move the kuei, to transform the fixed emotion, so that the process of living can go on. The act of consultation focuses the bright spirit of the shen directly into the problem. It offers the knot of pain and compulsion a chance to be seen, to be mirrored in the symbolic order. It brings to light what is hidden and offers ways to deal with it. As the problem comes to light, we are released from its compulsive emotions.

SPIRIT AND SYMBOLS

Hsiang is the word for symbol, the tool used by the shen to move the kuei (see page 25). A symbol has the power to connect things, to connect them with the invisible world. The 64 Figures of The Book of Change are all hsiang. They were created by mediums and sages through a kind of imaginative induction that is also called hsiang. We can use the oracle to hsiang something and turn it into a symbol. You carry on the symbolic process called hsiang by imitating the symbol so that you become its image. We make the connection between the invisible world of the spirit and the visible world of our lives by playing with the symbols, by acting them out.

THE WAY OF THE HEART

The circle of Teachers whose practices are recorded in *Ta Chuan* recognized *The Book of Change* and its symbols as the most potent mediumistic tool in existence. They saw it as a way to radically transform awareness, open the heart and contact the helping spirits (*shen ming*) in the same way the ancient wu were able to contact them. Their *Great Work* or *Great Enterprise (Ta Ye)* was to articulate this way of the heart and pass it on to future generations. It is this power, the ability to feel the spirit at work, that is responsible for the continuing fascination *The Book of Change* has held for people both East and West.

THE FRIENDSHIP OF THE SPIRIT

Ta Chuan shows Change as opening up a potent, mysterious yet knowable world that you can enter through divination. This gives you a way to understand the transformations in the world we live in. It gives you access to "bright spirit" which will move and protect you while encouraging you to act out of the best parts of your nature. It is a personal and powerful way to experience the spirit, a way of transformation allied to earlier practices of mediumship and spirit possession. This experience of the "helping spirit" can make you sage—clear-seeing, knowing the mysteries of death and birth, feeling the friendship of the spirit and love for others.

I suggest that a group of early Taoist practitioners is the origin of both *Ta Chuan* and the practice of using Change as a means of spiritual transformation. They were engaged in a radical re-invention of the oldest practices of "talking with the spirits" in a very dangerous time. They offered a way toward peace and self-realization that responds to individual concerns and spreads spiritual well-being. This is the most powerful and perennial appeal of the book.

So the fourth figure in the "Vinegar Tasters," the ghost looking over Lao-tzu's shoulder, is like one of those early spirit-mediums, the women and men who were wu. This person can "see and hear what is occulted." She or he gives to "those above (shen) and those below (kuei) what is due to them." This generous power of discrimination causes a luminous spirit (*shen ming* or the light of the gods) to descend. As this spirit takes up its home within a person, he or she becomes "daimonic and clear-seeing," profoundly connected to the invisible world of the spirit.

For these early Taoists, divination with Change was a way to go to meet that spirit. Here are two statements from *Kuan-tz'u*, a text from about 400 BCE, that give a clear sense of this practice:

> *When your chi (life-energy) is on the Way,*
> *It vitalizes you.*
> *When you are vitalized, you imagine.*
> *When you imagine, you know.*
> *When you know imagination, you stop.*
> *The hearts of all beings are shaped like this.*
> *If your knowing seeks to go farther,*
> *You will kill them.*

This Figure says there is a limit to "knowing," and that limit is imagination. Change puts you on the way, vitalizes your imagining with its symbols, opens your heart and that is enough. Then the spirit arrives.

> *Look, there is a shen within your person.*
> *Now it goes, now it comes.*
> *No one can imagine it...*

> *But if you reverently clean its abode*
> *It will come of itself.*
> *You will recover your own true nature,*
> *It will be fixed in you once for all.*

In my opinion, this is the kind of Figure whose teachings compose *Ta Chuan* and its "New Way (Tao) of Divination." This New Way proposes that we, too, can be like the sage-mediums of old. We can use Change to refashion our imagination. We can call on the *shen*, the bright spirit, to take a place in our heart. As we go on with the work, the spirit will spontaneously arrive.

Keywords in the Great Treatise

These words introduce ideas, things, and thoughts that are important to Ta Chuan *and the world from which it came. They are things people argued about, ideals, characteristic ways of thinking, and important experiences. Words in bold are those most frequently used in this translation—whether Chinese or English. I've used certain Chinese words and expressions throughout because their meaning is too rich and complex to be fully realized in their English equivalents. However, where I've felt that the English word works better, for example Change, I've kept it.*

Change, *Yi* or *I*, is the most mysterious word of all. It is a quality of the world we live in, an inner, creative energy as well as the name of a divination book and the technique associated with it. It is also applied to the school that uses this mysterious quality as a spiritual Way.

The book and the processes called I or Yi actually contain many kinds of change. There are images of the orderly changes in nature (*p'ien*), like the seasons or the stages of life. There are images of transformation (*hua*), like water turning to ice, a caterpillar turning into a butterfly or a live person turning into a dead

person. There are images of cyclic alternation, like day turning to night or yin turning to yang. There are images of depletion, of exhaustion and of rebirth.

Though it includes these things, Change itself is something different. Its primary meaning is "trouble." It was first used to indicate sudden, disastrous storms, unexpected losses or times of political upheaval when confusion intervenes. Structures break down; something extraordinary happens. The world, in one way or another, reverts to chaos. It is a Time of Troubles.

Another meaning of Change shows the response to trouble: versatility, imaginative mobility, openness and ease. It suggests a fluid personal identity, a fertile imagination and the capacity to move with the breakdown of normal values. It is as mysterious, unpredictable and fertile as the Tao.

Through Change you can move as fluidly and unpredictably as the chaotic force it represents. The spirits and symbols of *The Book of Change* connect the Change of the universe to your own inner Change, your creative imagination, if you choose to use them.

Chün Tz'u or **Realizing Person** is an ideal of conduct, someone who has committed him or herself to the Way and the process of self-realization. I read its basic meaning as "the person who uses Change to follow the Tao and thus accumulate the power and virtue (te) to become who he or she was intrinsically meant to be."

The oldest meaning of the term is "nobleman" or "son of the chief." We see pictures of this Chün Tz'u in the Book of Poetry, dating back to 1000 BCE and the "Golden Age" of the Chou. The poems are very beautiful and graceful, and the portrait of the nobleman is striking. He is not simply powerful. He is beautiful, desirable, highly skilled and quite refined, capable of profound thought, noble behavior and self-sacrifice. There is a numinous glow around him that represents te. He is someone who fully expresses what it is to be human.

About 400 BCE Confucius appropriated and re-defined this word. He turned it into a moral term, whereby it came to mean someone who was perfected in his moral discipline. Confucius idealized the early or Eastern Chou (1100–c.700 BCE) and tried to "reconstruct" its rites and rituals as a basis for moral behavior. His discipline consisted of introjecting this set of rules and rituals until they became automatic. Someone who did this was "superior" to those around him and deserved to rule them, thus the common Western translation of Chün Tz'u as "superior man." These two meanings—"morally superior Confucian" and "one who uses Change to realize him or herself"—as well as the shadow of the numinous nobleman, all exist in the word Chün T'zu.

divination in the context of *Ta Chuan* means "yarrow-stalk divination," the use of 50 yarrow stalks and the collection of divinatory symbols called *I Ching*, *Chou I* or *The Book of Change*.

Historically, the earlier counterpart to yarrow-stalk divination used the carefully prepared shoulder bone of an ox or the undershell of a tortoise. A series of shallow depressions was scooped in the reverse side of the bone, then a red-hot bronze rod was applied to them. The face of the bone cracked in a particular way, and the diviner read the angle of the cracks. This form of divination, called scapulomancy, is associated with the Shang court. Spirit-mediums, dream interpreters, temple-block soothsayers and specialists in reading signs and omens were also active at the time *Ta Chuan* was composed.

Originally, divination was a way to ask the spirits if they approved of an action. It was used to time the great sacrifices and the activities of the king. It developed into a strategic tool, then became a method of spiritual transformation as it became available to people outside the royal courts. The creative

47

ferment and the very real dangers of the Warring States period led to a great interest in what divination is and does.

Gates of Change is a pair of words, **Ch'ien** and **K'un**, that symbolize the two Primal Powers as they exist within Change. They appear in the *I Ching* only as the names of the book's first two divinatory Figures. They are used as a pair for the first time in the *Ta Chuan*. Some of the possible meanings of Ch'ien and K'un are as follows.

Force/persisting, Ch'ien: spirit power, creative energy, forward motion; dynamic, enduring; firm, stable; activate, inspire; heaven, masculine, ruler; strong, robust, tenacious, untiring; also: exhaust, destroy, dry up, clear away. The ideogram portrays rising energy, the sun and growing plants.

Field/yielding, K'un: the surface of the world; concrete existence, the fundamental power to give things form; earth, moon, mother, wife, servants, ministers; supple strength, receptive power; welcome, consent to, respond to, yield, give birth, bear fruit; agree, follow, obey; nourish, provide, serve, work for. The ideogram for K'un portrays an earth altar.

These words connect with the many paired words that describe the two primary powers that interact to create the 10,000 things of the world in which we live: Heaven and Earth, dark and light, great and small, strong and supple, sun and moon, transformation and continuity. *Ta Chuan* suggests that all of the powers and changes in the world are imaged in the mysterious process called Change.

Great Work or **Great Enterprise, Ta Ye,** describes the process of spiritual transformation inherent in the new way of divination proposed by *Ta Chuan*. It represents an individual process through which you acquire a helping spirit and "become sage" a social process made up of "politically potent actions" through which the world can return to the Way; and the effort on the art of the practitioners of the new way to make it available to others.

gua literally means a pile of things, the pile of lines that make up what we call a trigram (three lines) or a hexagram (six lines). I translate the word as "diagram."

In *The Book of Change*, the six-line diagrams serve to organize and display the divinatory texts and give access to them through the process of consultation. They also have a weight and meaning of their own, an element in the interpretive process that shows the configuration of yin and yang energies.

The three-line diagrams, gua, eventually evolved from the six-line diagrams and became a complex interpretive tool in their own right. They became the *Pa Gua*, the Eight Diagrams, both the basis of a philosophical system and magical tool. This system, parallel to but not identical with that described in *Ta*

Chuan, is described in *Shuo Gua*, another part of the Ten Wings. Used throughout the later Chou period, it became the base for medical, scientific and divinatory techniques of "correlative " thinking.

In *Ta Chuan* there is a conflict between these two systems, a conflict that reflects the Confucian struggle to re-imagine a Taoist text. Confucians identified with the Eight Diagrams, for they provided a logical explanation of the meanings of Change that could be connected

OPPORTUNITY KNOCKS
The Eight Trigrams of the I Ching have become a universal symbol—here they border an ornate door-knocker on a Taoist Chinese temple in Penang, Malaysia.

to a social and moral myth. Coupled with line analysis, they allowed the construction of a cosmology that could fix the meaning of the mysterious words. An opening wedge in this re-interpretation was the statement that "in the beginning there were the Eight Diagrams."

49 ◼

heart or **heart-mind, hsin,** is the center of our being, the seat of images, affections, desires, intentions and will. This word is also translated as "mind," for the Chinese of the period believed that we think with our hearts. The heart spontaneously produces images, and these images shape our desire. They believed that if is possible to train the heart and waken its latent powers, including the Sage-Mind that lies deep within its depths.

As in many other things, Taoists and Confucians had and still have different ideas about what this training ought to be. Confucians would inscribe the rules of propriety in the heart and repress what opposes them. "Repressing yourself and returning to the rites is being human," Confucius said. Taoists would empty the heart of all these rites, so you can see the truth that emerges.

Heaven and Earth, *T'ien Ti,* is the name for universe, for everything that exists. It comes into being when the sky power and the earth power couple. One image for **T'ien Ti is** a turtle, happily swimming in the fertile waters of chaos. His upper shell is the overarching heaven above us, and his lower shell the flat earth beneath us. We, and all that is in our world, are the soft flesh in between. The specifically human world is called All-Under-Heaven *(T'ien Hsia).* I translate this as "the world we live in," and this concept crops up often in *The Book of Change.*

Early divination focused on learning the will of Heaven and the feelings of the royal ancestors who reside there. The Way of Heaven was the path that good men sought to follow, for "if you depart from Heaven, what good can you do?" Heaven-and-Earth connects with the long series of similar pairs describing the primal opposites. See *Gates of Change.*

kuei shen or **ghosts and spirits** represent the kind of non-human beings or psychic complexes that may be encountered during divination. Their interaction gives us an insight into how spiritual divination works. Kuei are malevolent spirits that belong to tombs and the earth. If you anger them, they are likely to haunt you. Shen are bright spirits They confer intensity, clarity, and depth on the soul. They also make Change work and can be "conjured" by its numbers. (See pages 42–43 for a fuller explanation.)

ming means both **fate** and **mandate**. The term's two meanings are both quite old, and they interconnect in a special way. As fate, ming shows us an individual destiny, marked off by the great limits of birth and death, given a texture by character and articulated through significant events. This fate is not implacable. But it is very hard to see, buried as it is in the body and the unconscious.

As mandate, the term ming shows us a clear command, often from *T'ien* or Heaven. Heaven's mandate *(T'ien ming)* is an important phrase. It is not just the power given by Heaven to an Emperor. It is an in-dwelling part of every one of us, the fate that Heaven has bestowed on you.

Divination, symbolic perception and imagination connect these two meanings. Through using Change and working with its symbols, you learn to recognize what Heaven asks of you. You can transform your fate into a mandate from Heaven. You become fully yourself and live in the Tao.

spirit-medium, wu, is the oldest religious figure in Chinese culture. A medium is different from a shaman. Mediums invite the spirit to enter and use their bodies and voices. They present the spirit to the human world. The activity of

the medium is often connected with a meal shared by humans, ancestors and spirits, during which the medium "embodies" the spirit or ancestor.

Change gives a symbol for such a meal in Hexagram 50, *Vessel* or *Ting*. Mediums also gave the spirits a voice in human affairs. They were regarded as the first sages, and probably produced many of the divinatory symbols collected in Change. The medium's function became an image of the act of divination.

sage and the **Sage-Mind** is an ideal of development, a person who has not only realized himself, but passed into ways of deep understanding usually unavailable to humans. In the oldest thought, a sage was a spirit-medium who had obtained the aid of a powerful helping spirit or *shen*. According to the Confucians, these sages were rulers who set up moral rules and organized culture.

Ta Chuan, however, suggests that there is a Sage-Mind that exists both inside and outside the flow of time. The ancient sages may or may not have been "real"

COOKING FOR THE GODS
The image for Hexagram 50, Vessel or Ting, is taken from these two-eared, three-footed bronze ritual vessels that were used for cooking food to serve to gods and ancestors.

51

people, but the mind that made them sage exists now as well as then. This Sage-Mind is identical with Change. The emergence of Change into existence is a product of the Sage-Mind at work.

Another aspect to this concept is that of the Sage People. Everything that is of worth in our world was generally seen as descending from the *Shen Jen* or Sage People, who lived in a time before even history began.

symbol, hsiang, is an image that has the power to connect things, to connect the visible world of your problem to the invisible world of the spirit. The 64 Figures of Change are all *hsiang*, created by a kind of imaginative induction that is also called *hsiang*. We can use Change to *hsiang* something, to turn it into a symbol. A *hsiang* is also a magic spell, a figure or likeness and a pattern or model. You can *hsiang*—enter into the symbolic process—by creating an image, imitating, acting, playing or writing. This leads to an important conclusion: we make the connection between the invisible world of the spirit and the visible world of our own lives by playing with the symbols, by imitating them and acting them out.

Tao means **"way"** or **"path."** In its oldest uses it denotes either a literal path or road or the life and behavior of a particular kind of person: a carpenter's Tao, a wife's Tao, a warrior's Tao.

It developed into the most fundamental, mysterious, and attractive term in Eastern thought, the "on-going process of the real" that traces a path for the entire universe and, at the same time, for every individual being within it. To be "in" Tao is to be connected to the source of meaning and value. A religious experience of a high order, it brings joy, connection, spontaneity, creativity and compassion. The basic divinatory signs of Change reflect this: "the Way is open" or "the Way is closed."

The word tao can be used to indicate the Way of Heaven and Earth, the Way of Change or the way of any particular thing. Confucians believed that Tao is cosmic order as it is reflected in a set of social regulations. Taoist belief sees Tao as a fertile chaos, a source of help and comfort. It is these two viewpoints that are reflected in two attitudes toward the word Tao that we meet in *Ta Chuan*.

***te,* power and virtue** or **potency,** is another very old word. It is closely associated with Tao, as in the *Tao Te Ching* or *Way Power Classic*.

Te is the power or virtue that allows something to fully exist. It is a kind of realizing power that people and objects can possess. It can be accumulated and nurtured. In the human world, it is the charisma or inner power that makes a "great person," a *ta jen*. Powerful te makes a powerful person. Exalted te makes a wise person or sage. Someone full of te is numinous because they have the power to realize Tao in their person. By accumulating and refining *te*, you become "great," that is, able to lead your own life. Change is a way to accumulate *te*.

transformation, hua, is a radical change of form. It marks a quantum change of energy, the move from one state of being to another. The most striking transformation is from life to death. Transformation crosses the boundaries. It marks when something changes shape. It is often coupled with another term meaning gradual change to produce the phrase *p'ien hua*, change and transformation. Gradual change leads to a sudden change of form (*hua*). For example, a human being slowly grows older day by day (*p'ien*) and finally dies (*hua*).

Transformation is of great interest to diviners, for the behavior of things in transitional states is exactly what they want to understand. If you locate a transformation, you know precisely where and how change is taking place. *Ta Chuan* connects transformations in the world directly to the calling (yao) or transforming (hua) lines of Change. When a line changes form from yang to yin or yin to yang, it pinpoints where transformation may occur in the situation about which you are inquiring.

wu wei or **not-acting** is the fundamental tool for coming into contact with the Way. It relies on the ability to dis-identify with compulsive passions, collective ideas and egotistic ambitions.

Wu wei is not simply sitting back and taking a passive approach to life. One of Taoism's central ideas is that you can create an empty space within yourself and, if you keep it empty, the Tao will appear in the fertile emptiness. Once the Tao is within you, you must move only when an impulse to act comes from this empty center. By doing this, you act in harmony with the Way and can spread peace rather than the conflict of battling egos. Without this capacity, what you do will come to nothing, because you are only acting out of your ego and its greed and hunger. The end result of such actions will inevitably be the opposite of what you had set out to do.

The Great Treatise

Introduction

Ta Chuan forms part of the central section of *The Book of Change*. Its main sources are what we might call Taoist or "Yi-ist," Confucian and Cosmologist, a tradition later used by all parties. It is divided into two parts that are roughly symmetrical but show quite different characters. The work as a whole was assembled from various sources and bears all the marks of an oral tradition. Each of the sections is a separate Teaching, a specific attempt to change the way we see reality. They are sometimes harmonious, sometimes conflicting, but they are not homogenous. Some preserve fragments of actual divinations in the Taoist or "Yi-ist" manner. Overall, *Ta Chuan* focuses on the spiritual and social importance of using the divinatory tradition called Change and the connection between its symbols and the dynamic processes that constitute reality, the "ongoing process of the real" or Way.

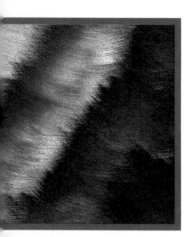

    Ta Chuan opens a big imaginative space, and it does this by using words in a special way that breaks down our usual attempts to categorize things. This sort of magical thinking is exemplified above all in the creative use of the word Change (*yi*). This word has several different meanings. "Change," the usual English translation, is really inadequate. There are separate words for gradual or regular change, such as the change of the seasons; for the transformation of one thing into another, such as a caterpillar turning into a butterfly or water turning into ice; for the running down or running out of something, when life, for example, is exhausted. Change makes use of all these modes, but its nature is quite different.

    At base, Change means "trouble"—unpredictable and destabilizing change. The term was first used to describe sudden storms that ruined crops, loss through theft or political breakdown.

It also suggests the way to deal with this trouble: imaginative mobility, ease, flow and a fluid identity. This is what we call spirit or creative energy, and what the ancient sages called Tao. The world works this way. It is the way of the spirit. It does not move through regular, predictable change; it moves through sudden, unexpected quantum leaps. If you want to survive, you must be able to move with the sudden change of symbols.

The second meaning of Change is a particular quality of mind, an irrational, intuitive, spontaneous quality that can go straight to the heart of issues. Taoists call this quality of mind "uncut wood," the "uncarved block" (p'u), or "Mr. Hun-tun," the original chaos. This points at something that quantum physicists exploring the brain have recently discovered. The creative core of our ability to make sense of things is a fertile, seething chaos. That chaos is Change.

A third meaning of Change refers to the name of a book and a divination technique that uses the book. *Chou Yi* or, to use its later name, *I Ching* is *The Book of Change*. This book and technique carried the myths and symbols of the ancient sages, for it was a way to understand how the spirits (*shen*) were moving. It could, in fact, connect you with the shen.

The mystery and power of this text is that the single word Change (yi) always implies all of these things at the same time. Change is the book, the technique, the cosmic creative power and our own fertile inner chaos. The symbolic use of the word Change links a spirit power in the world, our inner creative vitality, and a technique of divination. Through the divination book, then, and the understanding that *Ta Chuan* gives us, we can contact creative energy in the world and in ourselves.

Part One

Understanding Change

Part One, Understanding Change, has a pronounced Taoist flavor throughout. It is a coherent exposition of the importance of understanding and using *The Book of Change* and an exploration of its nature—its spiritual significance and connection to the Way—and how its symbols work to effect that connection. There is a consistent emphasis on the importance of the words of the oracle, and the effect they have when you "turn and roll them in your heart." It shows how *The Book of Change* doubles all the processes that create the reality we experience (1.1); tells us how to become a Realizing Person and set our feet on the Way (1.2); explores the nature of the words, lines, diagrams and symbols (1.3); shows how Change connects with the Sage-Mind and includes all other schools of wisdom (1.4 & 1.5). Understanding Change also gives us an idea of how the oracle "speaks," meditative directions on fixing it within us and an idea of the goal of the process (1.6 & 1.7 & 1.8). It explains the number magic of its consultation method (1.9); gives a series of divinations with the Master (1.10); and shows the nature of the Sage-Mind it embodies (1.11). Understanding Change concludes by pointing at its creative power, the nature of the "spirit-things" it uses, the Great Enterprise of transformation it implies, and the trust it can inspire (1.12).

I

HOW CHANGE IS LIKE
HEAVEN AND EARTH

1.1

This is the first thing. Examine it carefully:
Heaven exalts things and raises them up.
Earth humbles things and lies beneath them.
In the same way Ch'ien and K'un
the poles of Change
determine the place of all things.

If you have understood this, then look around you:
Low lying and high standing things are spread over the Earth;
thus there are low places and high places in Change.
The alternation of moving and resting is constant in Heaven;
thus strong and supple lines decide Change.
Events never occur alone. They cluster together.
The reading in Change
comes from the spirit they belong to.
It shows when the Way is open and when it is closed.

Remember:
The changes and transformations of Heaven
are in the symbols of Change.
The changes and transformations of Earth
are in the forms of Change.
Everything is seen clearly in Change.

This is why the strong and the supple lines rub against each other,
why the Eight Symbols stir against each other,
always acting and reacting.
Change and transformation are drummed on
by the symbol of Thunder,
they are moistened by the symbols of Wind and Rain.
The symbols of Sun and Moon make their cycles,
bringing us heat and cold.

But the greatest forces are Ch'ien and K'un. Listen:
The process of Ch'ien completes things through the male.
The process of K'un completes things through the female.
Ch'ien knows the Great Beginnings.
K'un makes and completes all things.
Ch'ien knows the beginnings because it changes
spontaneously with ease.
K'un makes and completes all things because it is simple.
Because Ch'ien is easy, Change is easy to know.
Because K'un is simple, Change is easy to follow.
When Change is easy to know, a great affection arises within you.
When it is easy to follow, the Great Result comes forth.
Great affection lets you endure.
Results that come forth make you Great.
This is the enduring power and virtue (te)
of the Realizing Person.
When you know Change as easy and simple,
you can grasp the pattern of the world we live in.
By grasping the pattern of this world we live in,
you can always move to the perfect position.
You are released from sorrow and fear.

大
傳

How Change is like Heaven and Earth

This is a Taoist Teaching

This Teaching shows how Heaven and Earth (T'ien Ti), *the world and everything in it, are an exact parallel of the group of things called Change.*

Everyone who read this Teaching would know about Heaven and Earth. Heaven is above us. Its power exalts and separates things. In face of Heaven, each person stands alone. Earth is beneath us. Its power humbles and strengthens things. In face of Earth, we recognize what joins us together. Heaven and Earth are the limits of what is knowable, the primal powers. They are the limits of thought and, at the same time, the gates through which things come into being. Beyond the gates is the mystery.

Here we are told something new: the poles of Change, the signs Ch'ien and K'un, symbolically participate in the primal powers. So Change contains all the vital characteristics of Heaven and Earth: high and low, moving and resting, the signs of the spirits, the ability to show if the Way is open or closed, the alternation of day and night, the round of the seasons, the way of male and female. The energies that are at work in Heaven and Earth also drive the symbols of Change.

Recognizing this symbolic reality lets us see several very striking things. The first is the observation that "events never happen alone. They always cluster around a spirit." The symbols of Change let you see this spirit and tell if it bodes well or ill.

Next we are told that all the "changes and transformations" of Heaven and Earth are in the symbols of Change. "Change and transformation" *(p'ien hua)* is a standard phrase describing all the kinds of change that we confront in the world, both gradual and abrupt. "Transformations" are of particular interest because they represent radical change, the quantum leap. The symbols of Change let us see transformations in both Heaven and Earth because they contain their transformative power. The transformations can also be seen in the movement of the Eight Diagrams *(Pa Gua)*. These three-line figures contain the energy of natural processes: thunder, wind, rain, running water, sun and moon.

The fundamental symbols of Change are Ch'ien and K'un, the first two divinatory figures. They contain the power of Heaven and Earth and connect us directly with Change. Ch'ien knows the great beginnings of things because it can change (yi) spontaneously with ease (also yi). This ability to change direction quickly and effortlessly lets us know Change in our hearts. K'un makes and completes everything because it is simple. The ability to act without complication or pride lets us follow Change in life.

Change is the most potent and numinous thing in the world we live in, the "All-Under-Heaven" *(T'ien Hsia)*. We can open ourselves to its influence, through the technique called Change. Out of this connection come a "deep affection" and "The Great Enterprise."

"Deep affection" has two possible meanings. You may acquire the capacity to inspire affection and loyalty in those around you, something that has great survival value. Or, and this is my own interpretation, you may suddenly feel a deep love for the symbols and the spirits that free you from a life of compulsion and drudgery. Similarly, the word "Great" is used in a double sense. On the one hand it means important, large, noble or potent action; on the other it means the ability to lead your life, to be an independent, free individual who "knows for himself whether the water is cold or hot." This is indeed a "Great Enterprise."

The symbolic participation of Change in everything around us, a participation that makes it "easy" to follow, has another result. Becoming aware of symbolic reality teaches you to see the pattern *(wen)* of things. You can take a "middle position" no matter what happens around you—a place between the strife of opposing feelings. Being in the middle is the first step toward freedom from compulsive emotions, from the fear of anticipation and sorrow over the unexpected. Change gives you direct access to the symbolic world behind appearances.

BECOMING A REALIZING PERSON

1.2

Sages set out the diagrams
so we could see the symbols behind them.
Sages attached words to make clear
when the Way is open and when the Way is closed.
Sages showed how the strong and supple lines push each other on
to create changes and transformations.

Because they saw all this they set up the signs to protect us.
The Way is open and the Way is closed
are symbols of failure and success.
The words about repenting, or shame and confusion
are symbols of anxiety and apprehension.
The change and transformation of the lines
is the symbol of advancing and withdrawing energy.
Strong and supple replacing each other
is the symbol of the alternation of day and night.
The six lines moving trace the way
of the three great pivots, Heaven, the Human, and Earth.
Because Change contains these powers,
the person who seeks to understand and follow it
can take his place in the moving world
and find tranquillity in the symbolic order.

This is what you must do.

First purify yourself and pose your question.

When Change responds to you:

Take joy in the words and roll them in your heart.

Let them move and change you.

Thus you find your place. The hidden symbol arises

as you roll the appropriate words in your heart.

Whenever you wish to move,

watch the transformation of the lines

and roll the divinatory signs in your heart.

In this way you become a Realizing Person. Heaven will aid you.

The Way will be open

and there will be nothing that is not advantageous.

Becoming a Realizing Person

This is a Taoist Teaching

Scholars like to say that the Chinese have no mythology. This usually means that they cannot find the sort of huge epic narratives full of heroes that they are used to in Western culture. It is true that Chinese myths don't tell stories. Rather, they point at something that acts like a door into "myth-time," the place where the stories are born.

This Teaching is about one of those "doors into myth-time," the idea or archetype of the ancient sages. The time before history began and the deep wisdom of the beings who lived there was something that few traditional Chinese doubted. When the ancient sages did something, it exuded insight and compassion. It was a founding action, from which benefits flow like water from a mountain spring. Further, the ancient sages lived in a Golden Age and whenever we use their words or imagine their being, the Golden Age returns. It is not confined to a specific place in time, nor a specific group of people. Any one of us can open the door.

This Teaching shows us how Change works and, most important, gives us a key to using it as a way of self-transformation. In the beginning, Sage People, probably diviners working with *wu* or spirit-mediums, set out diagrams of Change. The diagrams help us see or intuit the symbols behind them, hidden deep in the imagination.

The Sage People realized that the transformations of the twin powers could be seen in the lines of the diagrams. Like birth and death, these transformations open and close the Way or Tao. They bring good times or bad times to people in the world we live in, the All-Under-Heaven. The Sage People attached words to these lines from their store of songs, omens, chants and warnings. They did this to help and protect us. This was the creation of the language called Change. It is the gift of the spirits and the Sage People who are virtually spirits themselves.

Because of them, Change contains the secret of advancing and withdrawing energy, the alternation of dark and light and the Three Powers or pivots—Heaven, Humanity and Earth. Because of the Sage People, Change can help us take our place in this moving world and find tranquillity, a heart at peace with itself.

The key to the process is divination. The mediating power is words. Whenever a problem, a difficulty, or an emotion arises, you must pose the question to Change in words. Then you must take the words of the answer into your heart. When you "turn and roll the words in your heart," the hidden symbol governing your situation will spontaneously arise, like a spirit that has been evoked. If you must move or act, focus on the words and signs of the transforming or "calling" lines *(yao)*. As you turn and roll them in your heart, an image of the best way to act will spontaneously appear.

This is not a logical process. It acts in the soul or imagination and it changes the way you think. You must be open to Change. By practicing this sort of divination, you set your foot on the Way. You become a Realizing Person, someone who is becoming who they are meant to be. Heaven will come to your aid. The Way will open before you.

WHAT THE WORDS SHOW

The Image speaks about symbols,
which connect us to the invisible world.
The lines speak about transformations,
which show spirit advancing and withdrawing.
The Way is open and the Way is closed speak about loss and gain
through a particular course of action.
Repenting and shame and confusion speak about small
defects corrected by a change of heart.
Without fault speaks about being skilled
at recovering from transgressing the limits.
We can look for strong and supple positions
in the diagrams and in our lives.
We can look at how Great and Small are related
in the diagrams and in our lives.
But our ability to know if the Way is open or the Way is closed
is present only in the words.
Our anxiety over repenting and shame and confusion
lies in our innate desire to stay within the limits of the Way.
Our feeling of being stimulated by being without fault
lies in the joyful experience of reformation.
The figures are Great and Small
so the Realizing Person will know how to act.
The divinatory signs point at danger and ease.
It is only the words that show
where your actions might lead you.

What the Words Show

This Teaching is common to all

This Teaching looks at some of the words of the oracle, the "attached words" that we "turn and roll in our hearts." The words are of critical importance. They can tell us where our actions might lead. The words connect us to Change.

The Image *(T'uan)* contains the first words we encounter. The Image is a group of words attached to the divinatory figure. The first word of this group was seen as the name of the Figure as a whole. These words connect us with what is happening behind the scenes in the potent invisible world. The words reveal the symbols.

After the Image, we see the gua or six-line diagram. Each of the six lines has a text attached to it. Due to a procedure in the consultation process, any of these lines may be designated as "transforming" or "calling" (yao). When a line "transforms"—when it turns into its opposite—the words attached take on great importance. They "call" out to us where and how spirit is changing shape, so we know how to act.

The divinatory signs the Way is open *(ch'i)* and the Way is closed *(hsiung)* are unique to Change. They are used throughout its texts. These signs tell us about possible loss and gain by showing whether the Tao is flowing or blocked. Other divinatory formulae, repenting, shame and confusion and without fault, show defects in our character which may arise if we act in a particular way. They speak to our innate moral center.

The position of strong and supple lines helps us know whether our place in life is Great or Small. Great and Small are key words, the oldest terms for yin and yang. Through them we know if we should be forceful and follow our own idea, or be flexible and yield to others.

Change implies that we have an innate desire to stay the Way, that we feel joy in finding it and returning to it. The attached words tell us if the Way is open or closed. They reveal what the fruits of our actions may be.

69

THE SAGE PEOPLE, THE SPIRITS, AND CHANGE

1.4

Change contains the measures of Heaven and Earth.
We can use it to stay in complete alignment
with the Way of Heaven and Earth.
Change looks up to include the signs in Heaven;
it looks down to see patterns on Earth.
It offers us knowledge of what is dark and obscure
and what is light and clear.
Where these two are one is the source of all beginning.
The Sage People who made Change
went to this great beginning
and returned to trace the ends of things. Through Change
they offer us the knowledge of death and birth.
Listen: The seed we see in a symbol
unites with body-energy
through the Earth's power of realizing.
This is what creates the beings.
A being is born from a symbol.
When the soul wanders, detaching itself and floating up,
a transformation occurs. This is death.
Through the symbols and the transformations
we can know the spirits and the ghosts,
and their appearance and desires.
Spirits come from symbols.
Ghosts come from transformations.
This is how all beings come into life and leave it,
through union and separation of the light and the dark.

Because the sages' understanding of Change
fully participates in Heaven and Earth,
the Realizing Person cannot go astray.
Change is a teacher without a peer.
Look: The Way of Lao-Tz'u is in it.
The knowing of the Sage People
continually encompasses the myriad beings.
It gives help to everything in the world we live in,
so the person who uses it will never step outside the Way.
Confucius and the ancient sages are in it.
Sage People made Change.
They always act from the sidelines.
They are never carried away
by the compulsive flow of desire.
Because they found joy in Heaven and in following fate,
the Realizing Person can be free of care and sorrow.
Those who preach retreat from the world, humanity, morality,
and loving others—all this is in Change.
The people who made and used Change
brought security to those who depended on them.
Their humanity was deep and profound.
They incarnated these qualities in their oracle.
Thus the Realizing Person acquires the ability to love.
So remember:
Using Change lets you embrace and encompass
all the transformations of Heaven and Earth,
with never a false step.
Using Change lets you mingle with and complete
all the myriad things, leaving nothing out.
Using Change lets you penetrate the Way of day and night
and comprehend it fully.
Thus the spirits are not confined by your thoughts
and Change is not confined in your body.

大
傳

The Sage People, the Spirits, and Change

This is a Taoist Teaching

This Teaching shows how Change encompasses the limits of being. It goes back to the "source of all beginning." It shows us what living and dying mean. The ancient Way of Change encompasses all that is important in the "Hundred Schools," the philosophers disputing the nature of the Way in the contentious and creative time when Ta Chuan *was made.*

Change contains the measures of Heaven and Earth. So we can use Change to "measure" our experience. It also contains the "signs" of Heaven and the "patterns" of Earth. That means it can offer us knowledge of what is light (Heaven) and what is dark (Earth). Thus it unites all opposites.

This union of opposites is the limit of the world. Those who made Change went to this great limit "where the two are one." Because they were sages and great spirit-mediums, they could trace the paths of all creatures from birth to death. We owe a great debt to these unknown and unnamed people who traveled into the mystery beyond dark and light. They offer us a forbidden teaching, the knowledge of birth and death.

These spiritual travelers saw that all things are born from a symbol (*hsiang*). A symbol is a heavenly spirit that unites with body-energy (*ch'i*) by using the realizing power of Earth (*K'un*). They became aware of the fact that symbols and symbolic reality create everything that lives on Earth.

At death, the being transforms or changes shape, just like a line in Change transforms from yang to yin. Being goes into hiding, back into the invisible. The Earth-soul (*p'o*) detaches from body-energy and wanders the Earth. The spirit-soul (*hun*) begins its journey back to Heaven. These are the two kinds of invisible beings we meet: spirits (*shen*) connected with Heaven, and ghosts *(kuei)* wandering the Earth. These are natural phenomena. If we understand their earthly or heavenly nature, we know how to deal with them. This is a very important teaching. It can free us from fear.

This lesson on ghosts and spirits *(kuei shen)* and the limits of our world illustrates that Change is a teacher without a peer. It penetrates all mysteries. By using it you cannot go astray. It contains the measures of Heaven and Earth, dark and light and birth and death. It contains the wisdom of all the teachings current in 400 BCE, the great names of Chinese culture: the Taoist teachings of Lao-tz'u and Chuang-tz'u; the Confucian ethics of Kung-fu-tz'u (Confucius) and Meng-tz'u (Mencius); the universal love of Mo-tzu; and the radical individualism of Yang Chu. From Lao-tz'u we learn to follow the Way; from Kung-fu-tz'u we learn the model of conduct provided by the ancient sages; from Mo-tz'u and Yang Chu we learn retreat, care and love. We find them all in Change.

This knowledge comes not through study and diligence, but through affection, dialogue and divination. Using Change lets you walk the paths of Heaven and Earth without one false step. You move with the rhythm of day and night. If Change can encompass so much, give so much and enable you to see so much, it is obvious that its spirit *(shen)* is not limited to your thinking and that the phenomenon of Change is much more than what happens to your body. Be aware. You are facing an extremely potent and far-reaching power.

易

WHAT THE SPIRITS ARE

One dark (yin), one light (yang), this is the Way.
To follow this tells you what is good.
To completely identify with it shows you what is essential.
If you want to be benevolent, call it benevolence.
If you want to be wise, call it wisdom.
People use this every day without knowing it.
Using tao to realize yourself is what is rare.
Look, you can see it in benevolence. It is the gift of life.
It is concealed in everything you do.
It rouses the Myriad Beings to live and act.
It does not share the Confucian philosopher's
anxiety about imperfection.
Its power and virtue are complete.
Its greatness possesses all things.
Through its great possessions it bestows prosperity.
Through its great power and virtue it renews life each day.
Now listen very carefully:
As the birth of all births, this Way is called Change.
Change is made of symbols.
What moves and completes the symbols is called Ch'ien.
What unfolds them into patterns of living is called K'un.
What shows our fate through these symbols is called divination.
Penetrating the transformations is called the work.
What we cannot understand in terms of dark and light
is called spirit.
As we do the work, the spirit arrives.

What the Spirits Are

This is a Taoist Teaching

This is one of the most powerful Teachings, an opening of the mystery of the Way that is both beautiful and radical. The first thing we are told is that "one light, one dark" is the Way. This became a very famous formulation. It is the first time in Chinese philosophy that the terms yin and yang appear as a pair.

This formula shows that nothing exists alone. Everything is a continual interplay: light and dark, life and death, joy and sorrow, love and hate, man and woman, expansion and contraction. In human life these qualities are constantly moving, first one, then the other: "one light, one dark." If you can totally identify your thinking with this process, never trying to hold one or the other, you have found the essential. You have found the Way. You can call it anything you want. It is not limited by names. It is in every action. We all use it to stay alive. What is rare is that someone uses it consciously to become what they are really meant to be.

The Way gives life. It gives quality to life. It rouses things to action. It lives and moves, totally ignoring the moral qualms of a Confucian philosopher. The Way, which we find by embracing the two in the one, has ultimate *te* (power and virtue). It is so great that it renews the whole world each day.

The Way has a great secret: as Change it gives birth to everything that has a beginning. Change and the Way are the same thing: the power that moves the symbols and the power that unfolds them into life. So divination with Change shows us how the symbols are unfolding to create our fate. We work with them to understand how to live and die. Even in death something is left, something mysterious we can't understand in terms of the dark and the light. That something is called spirit (*shen*). As we do the work, the spirit arrives.

THE VOICE OF CHANGE

1.6

Change is broad and great.
If it is asked to speak of what is far, it encounters no obstructions.
If it is asked to speak of what is in the soul,
it is calm and correct, unmoved by personal desire.
When it speaks of what lies between Heaven and Earth,
everything is presented.
I will tell you how it works:
First, there is Ch'ien. At rest, it is alone and concentrated.
In motion it is straight.
This is how what is Great comes into being.
Then there is K'un. At rest, it is infolded. In motion it opens out.
This is how what is broad and vast comes into being.
Through being broad and Great,
Change matches Heaven and Earth.
Transforming and continuing, it matches the Four Seasons.
Impartial and fitting, embodying both dark and light,
it matches the Sun and Moon.
Through being inherently good, easy and simple,
it matches the highest power and virtue.

The Voice of Change

This is a Taoist Teaching

Here, Change is equated with what is broad and what is great. These two qualities are linked with the primary energies Ch'ien and K'un. Through Ch'ien, Change can speak of what is far, the outside. Through K'un, Change can speak of what is near (nei), *the inside or what is in the soul. Change encompasses Heaven and Earth and everything that takes place between them.*

We learn something here about how Ch'ien and K'un move. At rest, Ch'ien, or creative energy, is alone and concentrated in itself. When it moves, it moves in straight lines. K'un, or structural energy, folds in on itself when resting. When it moves, it unfolds or opens out. Change matches both these energies. It matches Heaven and Earth, the Four Seasons, and the Sun and Moon. The word "matches" indicates that it is the same category of being, and partakes of the same kind of energy. Because it is good, easy, and simple, Change contains the most powerful *te* in the world.

The point, however, is that it must be asked to speak. Only an important question by a particular individual can set this potency into action. Once asked to speak, Change encounters no obstacles because it is unhampered by desires or prejudices. It can present you with an image of anything in the world we live in. Ch'ien moves and gives you a symbol; K'un unfolds it into a pattern of life.

易

大傳

ERECTING THE GATES

1.7

One day the Master said: "Is not Change above all other things?
Sages use Change to exalt their power and virtue
to include the power of Heaven.
They broaden their field of understanding
to include the strength and expanse of Earth.
The intuition of Heaven raises us up.
The things that connect us with others humble us.
Through exaltation we follow Heaven.
Through connection we follow Earth.
Give Heaven and Earth their fixed places within you.
Erect the Gates.
Then the transformations can take place between them.
This is what will complete your nature.
It will sustain you and let you endure.
It is the Gate of the Way.
It fixes the heart and frees you from compulsion."

Erecting the Gates

This is a Taoist Teaching

Here we meet the Master. I believe this is a real voice, a Taoist master of about 400 BCE, giving instructions to a group of students studying Change as a means of spiritual transformation. It is a voice reaching across the centuries to give us, too, the gift of the Way.

These are basic instructions. First, there is proper value. You must realize that Change, as philosophy and as practice, is superior to other methods of spiritual transformation. Sages used it to exalt their power and virtue and to broaden their field of understanding. They connected their virtue with Heaven and their understanding with Earth. This moved them out of the petty wrangles of the ego.

The Master explains what Heaven and Earth do: heaven is intuition. Connection to Heaven raises us up and exalts us. Through Heaven we find our mission. Earth is thought, thought that connects us with others. Through Earth we find a place in the world.

We must give these two fundamental powers fixed places within ourselves. This is a kind of inner discipline that opens up the Way for Change. We must "erect the gates." Then the process of transformation begins.

By doing this, you "fix your heart." You no longer run here and there after each emotion. It is not that you repress your feelings, you dis-identify with them. Change will help you do this. By realizing and fixing the poles within you, you can complete your own nature or fate.

易

大傳

THE SAGE-MIND, THE SYMBOLS, AND THE LINES

1.8

This is what the Master said one day as he contemplated Change:
"The Sage-Mind has power to see into the mysteries
of the world we live in.
The Sage-Mind can spontaneously imitate
their forms and qualities and produce symbols.
The symbols fit all the individual properties
and participate in the mystery
of what cannot be directly known.
This is why the figures in Change are called symbols.
The Sage-Mind has the power to see all movements
in the world we live in.
It observes how things meet and what spirits are involved.
It spontaneously produces guides
and attaches divinatory signs
to tell us when the Way is open and when the Way is closed.
These guides are called the lines.
Through the symbols we can speak of the most terrible things
that can be contemplated, without arousing fear or disgust.
Through the lines we can speak of the most fluid possibilities
without producing confusion.
Observe them carefully and they will speak to you.
Deliberate over them and they will move you.
By observing and deliberating over an answer from Change,
your transformation is spontaneously completed."

One day Change said to someone:
"A calling crane in the dark.
Her son is in harmony with her.
I have a beloved wine-cup.
Associate with me, I will simply pour it out.
(Hexagram 61 *Conforming to Center*)

The Master explained: "A Realizing Person sits in his room.
His words go forth.
When these words are good
there will be resonance for a hundred li.
From nearby it will be much stronger!
A Realizing Person sits in his room.
His words go forth.
When these words are not good
there will be opposition for a hundred li.
From nearby it will be much stronger!
Like the calling crane, words issue from your being
and stimulate others.
Actions come from within you and are manifested far away.
Your own words and actions
are the pivot and trigger of this situation.
The pivot and the trigger of your own words and actions
will determine your honor or disgrace.
A Realizing Person can move Heaven and Earth
with his words and actions.
Shouldn't you be cautious with these powerful tools?"

One day Change said to someone:
Concording people first cry out and sob, and then they laugh.
(Hexagram 13 *Concording People*)

The Master told him:
"The Way of a Realizing Person flows out or is blocked,
speaks or is silent.
But when two companions are one in heart,
their strength breaks iron,
and their words are fragrant orchids."

One day Change said to someone:
Offer a sacrifice using a mat of white thatch grass.
Without fault.
(Hexagram 28 *Great Exceeding*)

The Master told him: "Normally it is sufficient
to lay the sacrifice on the ground.
Instead you use a mao-grass mat.
What inauspicious sign could come from this?
Mao-grass itself is trivial,
but how it is used is very important.
If you use this kind of caution and craft to move
there will be no error."

One day Change said to someone:
Humbling, humbling.
A realizing person uses this to step into the Great River.
The Way is open.
(Hexagram 15 *Humbling*)

The Master told him: "Work without boasting.
Acquire merit without displaying your virtue.
This brings superlative power and virtue,
for you have never placed yourself below others before.
Such power and virtue will be filled.
Such conduct will be revered.
Thus you can establish your position."

One day Change said to someone:
An overbearing dragon, there will be repenting.
(Hexagram 1 *Force*)

The Master told him: "Noble but in the wrong place!
Standing high with no following!
Does not assist able people below him!
Your every move brings cause to repent."

One day Change said to someone:
Do not issue forth from the inner door and chambers.
Without fault.
(Hexagram 60 *Articulating*)

The Master told him: "When disorder begins,
the first steps are always words.
If the prince is not discrete,
he will lose his minister.
If the minister is not discrete,
he will lose his life.
If plans are not kept secret,
their completion is injured.
Therefore, be cautious, be silent and do not expose yourself!"

One day Change said to someone:
Bearing a burden and riding in a carriage.
This will invite outlaws in the end.
Shame and confusion.
(Hexagram 40 *Loosening*)

The Master told him: "The makers of Change
knew about robbers and outlaws:
'Bearing a burden and riding in a carriage
invites outlaws in the end.'
Listen to me: Carrying a burden is a commoner's job.
Riding in a carriage marks a noble.
When a commoner rides in a noble's carriage,
it makes the outlaws immediately think of robbing him because
he is out of place.
You insult those above you and oppress those below you.
You are isolated and robbers plan to attack.
A careless guard tempts thieves,
just as luxurious ornaments rouse lust.
Listen to what Change says and think about it very carefully:
'Bearing a burden and riding in a carriage
invites outlaws in the end.'
This is an invitation to steal. You are flirting with disaster."

The Sage-Mind, the Symbols, and the Lines

大傳

This is a Taoist Teaching

Here again we hear a Master speaking. This teaching is on the "Sage-Mind," our innate capacity for enlightenment and wisdom, and its relation to the symbols and the calling lines of Change. The focus is our individual salvation.

The "sage" and the "Sage-Mind" are controversial. Sages represent a Golden Age before history began. Everything of worth was felt to flow from this source. But the identity of these sages was a topic of bitter debate. For Confucians, the "sage" is a culture-hero who brought order to the world and created hierarchical civilization. Taoists, on the other hand, saw the "sages" as living before the advent of the culture heroes who, they felt, destroyed morality, value and happiness.

The Master is talking about a Sage-Mind that exists outside the flow of time and space. This moves the question of origins and invention into imaginal rather than literal reality. The Sage-Mind is a quality of imagination that we all share. It has the power to recognize spirit and to "symbolize" it—to bring forth a symbol that reproduces its power. The Sage-Mind explains the actions of the world by referring to the mystery that is beyond the everyday world.

The Sage-Mind cares for us. It demonstrated its care and affection by spontaneously producing the symbols and the lines that tell us if our Way is open or closed. By using these symbols, we can think of the most terrible things and not be frightened. We will be able to see into the most confusing possibilities and not be disoriented, for we can adjust to them. We will understand symbolic reality and the enormous power it possesses. These are the gifts the Sage-Mind gives us through Change. If we observe them, they will speak to us. If we deliberate over them, they will move us. If we use them, we will be spontaneously transformed.

大傳

The second part of this Teaching is a series of quotations from *The Book of Change* with spontaneous comments by the Master. The divinatory use of *The Book of Change* was a very important part of the spiritual discipline called Change. Tibetan monks still do this as part of their monastic life. I believe these examples represent actual consultations. The comments are directed to specific inquirers. This makes them doubly unique, for the answers would be different if different people were involved. These are unique divinatory portraits.

All the examples use texts associated with calling (*yao*) or transforming lines. There is no mention of other possible symbols or strategies. The lines must have been of primary importance, particularly when the question involved any kind of action.

Further, the comments on these answers are all spontaneous. There is no systematic analysis of number, line position or yin-yang relation, all part of a later Confucian school of analysis. The only tool here is the Master's capacity to respond to a symbol, to register the problem in the symbolic world. He does not analyze the line, he interiorizes it. He responds spontaneously, like the Sage-Mind he described. The technical analysis that so occupied later thinkers is nowhere to be seen.

易

易

大傳

THE GOAL OF CHANGE

1.9

Change makes the Way visible.
It shows spirit in action,
and helps you accumulate power and virtue.
Those who use Change receive aid.
They acquire a helping spirit,
like those who in ancient times were protected by the gods.
The Master asked one day:
"If you know the way of Change and the transformations, won't
you know how spirit acts?"

The Goal of Change

This is a Taoist Teaching

Here the Master speaks again. We can feel his characteristic brevity and his radical sense of what is important.

The Master states concisely that the purpose of this discipline is to acquire a helping spirit (shen) like the old shamans and spirit-mediums. Using Change can show you the Way. It helps you accumulate the power and virtue (te) to become an accomplished or individuated human being. If you know the way of Change and its transformations, the ways and actions of spirit are open to you.

NUMBER MAGIC AND CONSULTATION

1.10

Heaven is one, Earth is two,
Heaven is three, Earth is four,
Heaven is five, Earth is six,
Heaven is seven, Earth is eight,
Heaven is nine, Earth is ten.
Heaven has five numbers,
Earth has five numbers.
Complete the two sets with the five places
and each number will match.
Heaven's numbers total twenty-five,
Earth's numbers total thirty.
The total of Heaven and Earth's numbers is fifty-five.
These numbers tell you how change and transformation occur,
and how to activate the ghosts and spirits.
The great total of the yarrow stalks is fifty.
We use 49, with one to act as Witness.
To create the symbols,
divide the stalks into two groups
to symbolize and invoke the two powers.
This is how the spirit enters.
Take one stalk up from the left
and suspend it between your fingers
to symbolize and invoke the three operations,
Heaven, Earth and Human.
Count the groups by fours,

to symbolize and invoke the four seasons.

Put the remainders aside,

to symbolize and invoke the unique lunar months.

In five years there are two of these months.

Repeat the counting by fours and put the remainder aside.

Repeat the suspending operation. Repeat the counting operation.

Repeat the process five more times to give you the whole.

This is called the operation by three and five.

The extreme of Ch'ien's sticks is 260.

The extreme of K'un's sticks is 144. This gives 360.

It corresponds to the days of the year.

The total number of sticks

that represents all the lines in the two parts of Change

is 11,520. This corresponds to the 10,000 things.

Therefore operations by four establish Change.

Eighteen transformations complete the diagram.

The Eight Diagrams form the small completions.

We extend them to create the 64 Diagrams.

If we expand these through their associations,

we can encompass everything that happens in the world.

Change brings the Way to light.

It shows its power and virtue and its spirit in action.

Through Change you can come into harmony with things

and serve the spirit.

The Master said: "If you understand the way

of change and transformation,

you know how the spirit behaves!"

大傳

Number Magic and Consultation

This Teaching is common to all

This Teaching describes the process of consulting the oracle by dividing and counting out a set of 50 yarrow stalks (achillea millfolia), the original form of which is lost. I give its closest approximation. These stalks were thought to be shen or spirit-things, like the tortoise shells used in the earlier form of pyromantic divination. This is a very "easy" (yi) and highly individual way to work with the shen. It is much easier than pyromantic divination, which uses painstakingly prepared bones and tortoise shells in an elaborate ritual, or the full trance of the spirit-medium (wu).

This process begins by assigning the even whole numbers to Earth and the odd whole numbers to Heaven. This gives a meaning to the odd and even numbered places or lines in Change. Each of the primal powers has five numbers. Their totals, 25, 30 and 50, are thought to activate the ghosts and spirits *(kuei shen).*

To use this method of consultation, you must acquire a set of 50 yarrow stalks. After you have posed your question, you bring out the stalks and set one aside as the Witness. You then divide the bunch of 49 sticks in two piles. Pick up and "suspend" one stick from the left hand pile between your last and third finger, then count out the right hand pile in groups of four until you have a remainder of 1, 2, 3, or 4 stalks. Suspend that remainder between your third and second finger. Then count out the left-hand pile in groups of four, and suspend the remainder between your second and first finger. You will have a total remainder in your hand of either 5 or 9 sticks. Put these aside and repeat the whole counting process two more times. On the second and third divisions, you will have a remainder of 4 or 8. On the last or third repetition, count the number of piles of four in front of you. There will be 6, 7, 8, or 9. These numbers correspond to the four kinds of lines that make up a diagram: 6 is a transforming yin line; 7 is a stable yang line; 8 is a stable yin line; 9 is a transforming yang line. This first number indicates the first or bottom line of the six-line figure. Bring the 49 sticks back together, repeat the entire operation five more times, and you have made a *gua* or diagram that gives you access to the words and symbols. You will form two of the Eight Diagrams (that have three lines). These are the "small completions." By extending or doubling them, you create one of the 64 Diagrams. The associations to the diagram you produced create a web of images that lets you see what is happening all over the world.

This process serves to bring the power and the spirit of the Way to light. It helps you serve that spirit by being in harmony with its activities. If you understand this, you understand how the spirit moves.

Historically, this is a quantum leap in divinatory technology. Its "easy" quality will eventually put the power of divination into the hands of individuals rather than royal families. According to legend, it gave the Chou nobles an enormous advantage in their fight with the decadent Shang rulers. A gift of Heaven, it contributed directly to their victory.

KNOWING THROUGH CHANGE

1.11

Change has the four-fold way of the Sage-Mind in it.
The Sage-Mind creates sages.
Change honors its speech through the words,
so you can model your thought on them.
Change honors its movements through the transformations,
so you can model your actions on them.
Change honors its creative power through the symbols,
so you can model your imagination on them.
Change honors its insight into living through the divinatory signs,
so you can shape your desires through them.
When the Realizing Person wants to act,
when desire or anxiety arises,
he puts the question to Change in words.
Change takes up this charge and echoes it.
Like a great mirror of all,
neither far off nor nearby, neither inside nor outside,
dark or deep exist for it.
Thus you can learn of coming events.
The Master asked: "If Change were not linked
to the ultimate power in the world we live in,
how could it grasp all this?"

We carry out the operations of three and five.
These operations determine a transformation.
The numbers of stalks are divided and combined.

This completes the lines of Heaven and Earth.

If we carry the numbers to their limits,

we find all the possible symbols in the world we live in.

The Master asked: "If Change were not linked

to the ultimate power in the world we live in,

how could it grasp all this?"

Change is without conscious thought and acts without purpose.

Like the Way, it is still and unmoving.

If you stimulate it by asking a question,

it penetrates the causes of everything in the world we live in.

The Master asked: "If Change were not linked

to the ultimate spirit in the world we live in,

how could it grasp all this?"

Change enabled the Sage People

to penetrate the extreme depths

of what is hidden in the profound.

They thoroughly understood

the infinitely subtle beginnings of Change.

It is only through what is deep

that we can penetrate the purposes of the world we live in.

It is only through what is subtle

that we can complete the workings of the world we live in.

It is only through our helping spirit

that we can hurry without haste

and arrive at our goal without going.

When the Master said,

"Change has the fourfold way of the Sage-Mind in it,"

this is what he meant.

大傳

Knowing Through Change

This is a Taoist Teaching

This is a Teaching on the identity of Change and the Sage-Mind, the Way of the "sage" that exists within each of us. The Master is one of the group of Taoist-oriented thinkers that turned Change into a spiritual Way in the fifth and fourth centuries BCE.

One of the most important things the Master does is to dis-identify the Sage-Mind from its manifestations. The Sage-Mind is a Great Way or capacity that exists independent of the categories of our thinking. And, like a spirit, it can be called, invoked or "accessed." The way to do this is through Change. The Master says Change contains the fourfold way of the Sage-Mind, and the Sage-Mind is what makes a person enlightened. He is proposing a double kind of imitation: Change "matches" the Sage-Mind, and we strive to "match" Change. This "matching" invokes the many meanings of the word symbol (hsiang), which include pattern or model, to imitate, to act, play or write, or to use your imagination.

We find the language of the Sage-Mind in the words of Change. We can model our thought on this language. We find the movements of the Sage-Mind through the transformations of Change (the transforming or calling lines). We can model our actions on them. We find the creative power of the Sage-Mind in the symbols of Change. We can model our imagination on them. We find the insight into living of the Sage-Mind in the divinatory signs of Change, so that we know when the Way is open or closed. We can shape our desires through these signs.

These words describe a transformation, whereby your ordinary mind is replaced by the Sage-Mind. This process only begins, however, when you "put the question to Change in words." It grows out of the events of your life and proceeds via the questioning of the oracle. This sets it off from simple philosophy.

Only when you do this does Change come to life. For Change is linked to the greatest potency (te) in the world we live in. It contains the symbols, the birth-seeds, of all things. We find them through the divination process. These 64 symbols can "grasp" any situation, letting you lay hold of it and understand your place in it.

Change does not act like a person. It acts like the Way. It is without conscious intention. Still and unmoving like the heart of a sage, when you pose a question it responds spontaneously. This is an important point. You do not just study Change. You use it. You experience it in the context of your own life. The charge of a human need or a heartfelt emotion will put it into action.

In the most ancient times, Sage People used Change to penetrate the extreme depths of what is profound. They used it to understand the subtle beginnings *(ji)* of change. Paradoxically, Change existed before the Sage People who created it or "set it out." The Sage People used Change to create Change. It exists both inside and outside of time.

We, too, can use it to acquire a helping spirit like those Sage People of old. That lets us "hurry without haste" and "arrive at the goal without trying." Both these phrases describe *wu wei*, the "not acting" or "not doing" so honored by early Taoists. It is actionless action where the spirit presides. This, we are told, is what the Master meant when he said Change has the fourfold way of the Sage-Mind within it.

"If it were not linked with the ultimate spirit in the world we live in, how could it possibly grasp all this?"

THE CREATIVE POWER OF CHANGE

1.12.1

One day the Master asked: "Change, what does it do?"
It opens and reveals how things exist.
It shows you how to fulfill desires correctly
and to do what you must do.
It does this and nothing else.
Sage People used Change
to penetrate the purposes of the world we live in,
to divine the courses of action in the world we live in,
and to settle all doubts in the world we live in.
Now listen: the power and virtue of the yarrow stalks is round
and invites the spirit;
the power and virtue of the diagrams is square
and tells you what can be known.
The meanings of the six lines transform
to give you insight into Change.
The Sage People used this to purify their hearts
and retire from the world,
hiding in the secret where mysteries begin.
They wanted to tell other people
when the Way was open and when the Way was closed.
The spirit gave them the ability
to know what was coming on the river of time.
Knowing this,
they could see and store up what has gone by.
Who could grasp this?

Those who were open and bright, intuitive and knowing,

they were warriors of the spirit without killing.

Change and the Sage-Mind are one.

They reveal the Way of Heaven,

the omens and the presence of the powerful ghosts.

They clearly discern all the forces at work

in our common human life.

From Change and the Sage-Mind,

Sage People brought forth the spirit things, the oracles,

anticipating what people need:

to understand their experience,

to feel the friendship of the spirit,

to live connected to the Way of Heaven.

Sage People used Change

like a spirit-medium purifies himself.

They fasted in order to raise their power and virtue

into the light of the spirits.

This is what they saw:

To close the gates of Change is called K'un.

To open the gates of Change is called Ch'ien.

One K'un, one Ch'ien creates the transformation.

This unceasing coming and going through the gates

communicates with all things.

What we can only see in the imagination is called a symbol.

What we can touch is called a vessel.

What we can use to regulate ourselves is called a pattern.

What helps us as it comes and goes,

so that all can use it,

is called the spirit.

大
傳

The Creative Power of Change

This is a Taoist Teaching

I have divided the very long last Teaching into four sections. Here in the first section, we are listening to one of the great teachers who turned Change into a spiritual practice. We can imagine him speaking in response to a question: What does Change do? The Master's answer is deceptively simple. Change, simultaneously a quality of mind, a quality of being and a divinatory technique, shows you how things exist and how you can fulfill your desires. These things involve discerning "fate" or "purpose." Sage People, who lived before history began, used Change like this. They used it to penetrate all the purposes and courses of action in this world and thus to settle all doubts, doubts that would lead to argument and conflict.

The power and virtue of Change is both round, which invites the spirit, and square, which grounds knowledge. Its six lines give you insight into how all things transform.

The Sage People used this power like spirit-mediums *(wu)*. They used it to purify their hearts and retire, hiding in the secret where mysteries begin. The spirit power they found there gave them the ability to "see" symbols on the river of time. This made them both seers and historians. They did this only because they were concerned for people. They wanted to be able to tell people when the Way was open and when the Way was closed, so they might live a better life. Who were these Sage People? Who could "grasp" such a great mystery? They were "warriors of the spirit who did not kill," bright, open and deeply intuitive.

Here, a great secret is revealed. The Sage-Mind and Change are one. They each show you the same thing: the Way of Heaven, the omens that show if the Way is open or closed, and the presence of powerful ghosts who must be dealt with. In our language this means they discern all the forces that influence human life. From the depths of the Sage-Mind, Sage

People brought forth the spirit-things that enable us to communicate with Change. They gave us all we need to live a good life: an understanding of experience, a connection to the Way of Heaven, and the friendship of the spirit.

Sage People found certain things they have passed down to us. The constant interchange of K'un and Ch'ien, dark and light, opens and closes the gates of Change. The ceaseless movement through this gate connects Change with all things. We should recognize a fourfold difference in the things we experience, though they have a common source. What we can only see, that is, see in imagination, is a symbol. It has the power to shape a situation though it is not yet manifest. What we can touch is a vessel or a tool. It gives us the power to realize and complete things. What we use to regulate our feelings, thoughts and behavior is called a pattern *(wen)*. What comes and goes throughout it all is spirit *(shen)*. It will spontaneously arrive to help us. Through Change it offers itself up for all of us to use.

THE SPIRIT THINGS

1.12.2

In order to help us know the spirit,
the sages invented the Great Axis:

▬▬▬▬▬▬▬▬

This brought forth the two First Powers:

▬▬▬▬▬▬   ▬▬ ▬▬

The two First Powers generate the Four Symbols:

▬▬▬▬   ▬▬ ▬▬   ▬▬ ▬▬   ▬▬ ▬▬
▬▬▬▬   ▬▬ ▬▬   ▬▬▬▬   ▬▬ ▬▬

Old or
transforming
yang energy

Young or
continuing
yin energy

Young or
continuing
yang energy

Old or
transforming
yin energy

The Four Symbols generate the Eight Diagrams:
The interaction of the Eight Diagrams into figures
determines whether the Way is open or closed.
Knowing this generates the Great Enterprise,
the work of self-transformation.
There are no greater originating symbols
than Heaven and Earth;
we see them in Ch'ien and K'un.
There are no greater transformations and continuities
than the Four Seasons;
we see them in the Four Symbols.
There are no brighter, light-giving symbols hanging from Heaven

than Sun and Moon;

we see them in the dark and the light lines.

There is no more honored social position

than the person of wealth and rank.

There is no greater maker of tools and vessels

whose use helps the world we live in

than the sage.

There is no greater way to encompass and understand

the myriad things,

to explore the hidden beginnings,

to penetrate what is deep,

to reach what is distant,

to know if the Way is open or closed in the world we live in, or to

create will and resolution

than the oracle.

So when Heaven created spirit-things

like the oracle,

Sage People took advantage of them.

When Heaven and Earth transformed,

Sage People imitated the transformation.

When Heaven hung down the symbols

that show if the Way is open or closed,

Sage People reproduced them.

They helped us to know all these things.

Change has four kinds of symbols

that act as omens:

opening, closing, the season and the time.

It is the words that are attached to the figures that tell you. They

determine if the Way is open or closed.

Then you are able to decide what to do.

大
傳

The Spirit Things

This Teaching is common to all

This part of the Teaching comes from the Cosmologists, thinkers who were trying to put together a coherent theory of the world expressed in diagrams. These diagrams were used to correlate all known phenomena on the basis of "association" or sharing a particular key quality. The very first phrases are common property. The Taoists also say that "The Tao gave birth to the One, the One gave birth to the Two, the Two gave birth to the Three, the Three gave birth to the Myriad Beings." The difference here lies in the movement toward the Eight Diagrams (Pa Gua). This sort of cosmological thinking was annexed by the Confucians in the Han Dynasty (226 BCE–220 CE) to create an "imperial" model of a closed and hierarchical world.

The Eight Diagrams are a fairly old way of interpreting the symbols of Change. As early as 600 BCE some diviners were using associations to these figures to help explain situations. There is a section of the Ten Wings, the Commentary on the Diagrams (*Shuo Kua*) that is devoted exclusively to enumerating and cataloguing the associations to these diagrams in particular.

Here they are used in a unique way, empowered as fundamental symbols of Change. Han Dynasty Confucians were extremely interested in the Eight Diagrams as part of a project to draw attention away from the words and symbols, which have multiple meanings, and focus it on the diagrams and lines, whose meaning could be fixed hierarchically. The myth of Fu Hsi, which we will see later, was also created at this time to prove that the Eight Diagrams were the most ancient part of Change. This, too, was a Han invention.

The rest of this Teaching enumerates the major points in the doctrine of using Change. There are a few innovations. After Heaven and Earth, the Four Seasons, Sun and Moon—great symbols of Change—we find "the honored social position of the person of wealth and rank." This is the beginning of a move that will turn the diagrams of Change into the signs of a fixed social hierarchy.

易

THE SYMBOLS OF CHANGE AND THE GREAT ENTERPRISE

1.12.3

One day Change said to someone:
Heaven shields his birth
The Way is open.
There is nothing for which this will not be advantageous.
(Hexagram 14 *Great Possessions*)

The Master explained:
"To shield means to protect and give help.
This is one who has found the spirit.
Heaven protects the flow of his life.
Humans give him help because he trusts this spirit.
He moves effortlessly in this spirit and reverences it.
He esteems what has worth.
Heaven shields his birth.
The Way is open.
There is nothing for which this is not advantageous."

One day the Master remarked:
"We all know that writing cannot exhaust
the many meanings of speech.
We all know that speaking cannot exhaust
the many meanings of thought."
We asked him: "Does this mean we cannot understand
the thought of the Sage-Mind that makes Change?"

The Master answered:
Sage People set up the symbols in such a way
that they bring out the meanings of the Sage-Mind.
They set up the diagrams to show you
what are and what are not your actual circumstances.
They attached words to these things
to fully bring out what they have to say to you.
They made the transforming and continuing lines
to show you fully what is advantageous.
Like spirit-mediums, Sage People drummed and danced
to bring down the spirits.
This happens to us when we use Change.
Remember this:
Ch'ien and K'un are the threads of Change.
Ch'ien and K'un set up the extremes
so Change can move between them.
Destroy the symbols of Ch'ien and K'un
and you could not see Change.
If Change vanished, Ch'ien and K'un would wind down
and the world in between them would cease to exist.
Change moves in and out of the moment called now.
What is upstream from the moment
we call the Way. It reflects the Ch'ien.
What is downstream from the moment
we call the vessel or tool. It reflects the K'un.
The moment of transformation and shaping we call Change.
The force that pushes all these things
into interacting with each other
we call arousing and stimulating.
Raising the process of knowing Change into awareness
and setting it forth for all the people to use,
that we call the Great Enterprise.

大
傳

The Symbols of Change and the Great Enterprise

This is another example of the Master's voice. By now, we have a sense of his character. He moves very quickly between different levels of thought. He has a wide range of experience. He speaks spontaneously and intuitively, circling around the same basic topics from different angles. He can move freely in time and is thoroughly comfortable with ambiguity. He has a real experience of the spirit and a thorough command of Change. He also shows a deep care and affection for those to whom he speaks.

Here the Master begins by elaborating on a calling line from Change. He uses it to describe someone who has found the spirit and flows effortlessly through life because of his wholehearted trust in this experience. The Master is pointing at someone who has "completed" the process of transformation. Heaven protects his birth in Change. The benefit spreads in all directions.

The Master then brings up the ever-present problem of language. Change, of course, exists primarily in written words. He first announces what is commonly accepted in Taoist circles: writing cannot fully convey speech; speech cannot fully convey thought. His disciples respond in consternation: "Does this mean we cannot understand the Sage-Mind behind Change because it is presented in written words?" The point is that the words of Change are not writing in the ordinary sense. They are "set out" through a hidden unity of diagrams, words, signs and lines that lets you "see." It reproduces the way the Sage-Mind knows. It is how the Sage-Mind creates meaning.

It induces an intuitive state in which other symbols spontaneously spring into awareness and you feel the Sage Mind at work. The Sage

People did precisely this when they "drummed and danced" to bring down the spirits into their body.

The Master then insists on the importance of setting up Ch'ien and K'un as the "threads of Change," the threads on the loom of time. Without these two poles, Change would vanish and the world would cease to exist. The stream or flow of time moves in and out of the moment we called "now." It flows from the future through the present into the past, moving from Ch'ien through K'un. Things that are upstream from the moment "now" exist as symbols or seeds, the creative potential of Ch'ien. Things that are downstream from "now" are vessels or tools. They exist through the realizing power of K'un. The moment "now," when things take on new forms, is Change.

There is a continual force forever pushing things on and bringing them together. It knows no stopping. It arouses and stimulates. What we are engaged on is the work of raising this force into awareness through the power of Change. We make it available to help people live their lives. This is called the Great Enterprise. It is what the Master is teaching.

易

I

易

TRUSTING CHANGE

By using the symbols,
Sage People saw all the spirit forces in the world we live in.
The symbols determine forms and appearances
and connect all things.
That is why they are called symbols.
Thus Sage People were able
to see and group
all the movements in the world we live in.
They examined how things met and stimulated one another
and they traced the ways that endure.
They attached words to distinguish
when the Way is open and when it is closed.
These words call out to you.
The underlying mysteries, the numinous situations
that run through everything in the world we live in,
are completely presented in the symbols.
Everything that stimulates movement
in the world we live in exists in the words.
How things transform and the shapes they take
exist in the transforming lines.
The forces that set these things in motion
exist in the continuing lines.
The light of the spirits exists in the people
who set out Change and in the Change they used,
silently completing the Way of Heaven.
It is an unspoken trust that carries and supports us
as we strive for the power and virtue
to become who we are meant to be.

Trusting Change

This is a Taoist Teaching

This beautiful reflection closes the first part of Ta Chuan. *It is about trust. It lays out the grounds on which we can trust Change. It asks us to make a commitment to Change as the single most effective way to live.*

The people who made Change used its symbols to see the spirit (*shen*) in the world we live in. The spirit not only determines the appearance of things, it connects the visible and invisible worlds. Change groups movements according to the spirit force behind them. It indicates how things interact and the paths that endure. The words tell you clearly when the Way is open and when it is closed. All the numinous situations, the mysteries that shape the world, are portrayed in the symbols. Everything that sets things in motion exists in the words. The shapes of their transformations are seen in the lines.

This is a complete parallel reality, a world of symbol and spirit. Not only can it predict what will happen, it induces spiritual transformation in those who use it. So a kind of trust binds the users and the founders of Change, those ancient sages who silently completed the Way of Heaven. The light of the spirit shines in this trust. It will carry and support you as you strive for the power and virtue to become who you are meant to be.

Part Two

Locating Change

Part Two, which I call "Locating Change," shows a struggle between a Taoist or "Yi-ist" view of Change and a Confucian attempt to redefine and fix it in terms of its own version of history and value. Many of the Confucian sections are late, being composed up to three hundred years after the Taoist re-imagining of Change was recorded. They seek to retroactively impose a quite different version of things.

     This Section tells us about Change and the Culture Heroes (2.1 & 2.2); how the world was split in two (2.3 & 2.4); gives a second series of divinations with the Master (2.5); tells how Change was created in a Time of Troubles (2.6); offers a way to accumulate te or power and virtue through certain of the Figures (2.7); tells us how to read Change by opening our hearts to its words; seeks to establish fixed values for line positions, exclude the participation of the spirits and connect Change directly to the Chou Kings (2.9–2.11); and states that harmony with Change can bring joy and peace to our hearts, open the thoughts of humans and spirits, and connect us to the Way (2.12).

CHANGE AND THE CULTURE HEROES

2.1 & 2.2

The Eight Diagrams are used to complete an arrangement,
thus the symbols are given a vessel.
Then the diagrams are doubled,
thus the lines are given a vessel.
Strong and supple push each other on,
thus the transformations are given a vessel.
The attached words give their commands,
thus movement is given a vessel.
The Way is open, the Way is closed,
repenting, shame and confusion
are warnings produced by this movement.
Strong and supple take up positions.
Their transformations and continuities
are created by the moment of time they portray.
Knowing if the Way is open or the Way is closed
is the fruit of divination.
The Way of Heaven and Earth becomes visible through divination.
The Way of Sun and Moon becomes clear through divination.
The movements in the world we live in
are gathered together by divination.
Ch'ien is completely solid in its aim and never doubts,

thus it shows us how to do things easily.

K'un is yielding,

thus it shows us how to do things simply.

This is what the lines echo. This is what the symbols reproduce.

Let the lines and the symbols move.

They show if the Way is open or closed.

The moment of time

that is the field of our action

is shown by the transformations.

The Sage-Mind is experienced through the words.

Fu Hsi and the Eight Diagrams

In antiquity Fu Hsi ruled the world we live in.

He looked up and saw the symbols hanging down from Heaven.

He looked down and saw the patterns on the Earth.

He saw markings on birds and animals

and the places where they lived on the Earth.

He drew on what was near within his body.

He drew on what was far.

He spontaneously brought forth the Eight Diagrams

to connect with the bright spirits

and to categorize the natures of the myriad things.

He was the first to use Change to help the people.

He invented knotted cords for counting

and nets and snares to hunt and fish.

Perhaps he used the symbol *30 Radiance* to do this.

The Divine Agriculturist, Shen Nung

When the clan of Fu Hsi was exhausted,
the clan of Shen Nung arose.
He split wood for a plow and bent wood for a handle.
He showed the world we live in
the advantage of plowing the fields.
Perhaps he used the symbol *42 Augmenting* to do this.
When the sun stood at the top of the sky he made a market.
He gathered all the people of the world we live in
and all the goods of the world we live in.
Exchange became easy (yi).
Each person left with what they wanted to have.
Perhaps he used the symbol
21 Gnawing and Biting Through to do this.

The Yellow Emperor and the Founders of Culture

When the clan of the Divine Agriculturist was exhausted,
the clan of the Yellow Emperor, Yao and Shun arose.
By comprehending the transformations in Change,
they made their people unweary.
They were transformed by the spirits
so the people respected them.
Change slowly builds up to cause a transformation.
By moving with the transformation, a new continuity occurs.
That is why Change says: "Heaven shields their origin.
The Way is open. There is nothing that is not advantageous."

The Yellow Emperor, Yao and Shun
let their garments hang down without binding them.
Thus there was peace and order in the world we live in.
Perhaps they used the symbols Ch'ien and K'un to do this.
They hollowed trees and boats.
They hardened wood in the fire as oars.
They showed the advantage of crossing streams
to open communication.
They reached what is far and benefited the world we live in.
Perhaps they used the symbol *59 Dispersing* to do this.
They tamed the ox, yoked horses together
and moved heavy loads to far places.
They benefited the world we live in.
Perhaps they used the symbol *17 Following* to do this.
They made double gates
and set out watchmen with wooden clappers
to prepare for violent visitors.
Perhaps they used the symbol *16 Providing for* to do this.
They split wood for a pestle.
They hollowed earth for a mortar.
Using mortar and pestle they benefited the myriad people.
Perhaps they used the symbol of *62 Small Exceeding* to do this.
They bent wood and strung it to make a bow.
They hardened wood in the fire to make arrows.
Thus they produced awe and fear in the world we live in.
Perhaps they used the symbol *38 Diverging* to do this.

The Sage People and the Officials

The first people lived in caves and forests.
Later, Sage People changed this to houses.
There was a ridgepole and a roof
sloping down to ward off wind and rain.
Perhaps they used the symbol *34 Great Invigorating* to do this.
At first the dead were buried
by covering them with thick brush in the wilderness.
No burial mound was raised. No trees were planted around them.
There was no time set off to mourn.
The Sage People changed this by using inner and outer coffins.
Perhaps they used the symbol *28 Great Exceeding* to do this.
At first, knotted cords were used to govern the people.
Sage People changed this with writing and documents
to govern the officials who supervised the people.
Perhaps they used the symbol *43 Deciding* to do this.
The power and virtue of Heaven and Earth gives us life.
The Sage-Mind is the Great Treasure
that lets us stand in the right place.
It allows us to help and protect other people.
Men are drawn by wealth.
But they are held by righteousness,
by giving, restraining and instructing.

大傳

Change and the Culture Heroes

This is a Confucian Teaching

This is the opening wedge in a new definition of Change. Though it is impossible to date this precisely, it is much later than the Taoist sections that articulate Change as a spiritual discipline. Here, someone is redefining what the Taoists have said. The spiritual message becomes social and hierarchical.

Once again we are told about the various parts of Change and what they can reveal, a set of qualities that has become familiar. There are, however, some important variations. This section opens with the Eight Diagrams (Pa Gua). It is the Eight Diagrams that "give the symbols a vessel." The phrase "giving something a vessel" means "helping" it to manifest in the physical world. Through the Eight Diagrams, the symbols, which are imaginal or spiritual, "unfold" into body.

This is a radical assertion. The assertion becomes even more aggressive when it is stated that "the diagrams are doubled [and] the lines are given a vessel." This maintains that the eight three-line figures came first; they have priority both historically and spiritually. The six-line figures that carry the texts are seen as being derived from the eight three-line figures. Historically we know this is simply not true. In the beginning were the hexagrams (gua); the three-line diagrams or trigrams (also called gua) evolved as a way of amplifying and interpreting the situation portrayed by the hexagrams. This was common knowledge among diviners. So why would someone claim otherwise?

Origins have a very high value for Chinese thinkers. The closer something is to the source, the more valuable it is. This Teaching is very carefully framed to reflect this. It begins with the assertion of the fundamental importance of the Eight Diagrams. It ends with an observation on how humans can be ruled by "righteousness" *(ji),* one of the key Confucian virtues. These poles are part of the "project" to define

Change in social terms and establish a myth of origins that connects it with ancient rulers who can be seen as predecessors of the Imperial state. We are presented with that myth, beginning with Fu Hsi and the Pa Gua and ending with the development of writing, in order to give instructions to government officials. All of this depotentiates the symbolic power of the words of Change, the prime focus of Taoist spiritual divination. It connects Change to the line of legendary sage-kings who, in the Confucian view, created culture—the idealized Golden Age of Confucian philosophy. People have puzzled over the ways that the inventions described can be seen as being inspired by the Figures that are mentioned. The key lies in trigram analysis and the associations to these three-line diagrams. This is a subtle but very important shift in thinking about how Change creates meaning. It shifts us from intuitive perception to analysis and from imagination to literal time and space.

SPLITTING THE WORLD

2.3

The ancient rulers were moved by Change
to invent many things.
Change provided symbols for this.
These symbols resemble many things and processes.
The Image is the basic thing that inspired them.
The lines showed the movement in the world we live in.
They used it to spread their thought.
They show how the Way opens and closes
and tell about repenting or shame and confusion.

Yang diagrams (trigrams) have more yin lines.
Yin diagrams (trigrams) have more yang lines.
What is the cause? Yang is odd, yin is even.
What is their nature? How do they act?
Yang has one ruler and two subjects.
This is the Way of the Realizing Person.
Yin has two rulers and one subject.
This is the Way of the Small Person.

Splitting the World

This is a Confucian Teaching

This Teaching is an example of a small thing with a long reach, an attempt to establish a moral dichotomy at the heart of all things. It splits things that have been joined in an equal but opposite relationship. Change is, of course, full of these: dark and light, heat and cold, high and low, contracting and expanding, Great and Small, yin and yang. One of the first developments of Confucian philosophy was a moralism that saw one of these sets of equals—yang, the Great, the male, the high—as morally superior to the other—yin, the Small, the female, the low. The world was split in two.

Here the leading edge of this wedge is inserted into Change. Yang, as the ruler, is identified with the "Realizing Person," a phrase used to identify someone who is following the Way. Yin, as the subject, is then identified with the Small Person who, by implication, cannot be following the Way. This duality—Realizing Person versus Small Person—is a new variation on the widening split in the world. It will, in the course of time, have enormous repercussions.

MEETING YOUR SPIRIT

2.4

What is pondering? What is care?

One day Change said to someone:
Wavering, wavering, going and coming.
Your partners will simply adhere to your pondering.
(Hexagram *31 Conjoining*)

The Master explained to him: "In the world we live in,
what is pondering? What is care?
In the world we live in, we all return to the same thing—death.
One result, many cares.
So tell me, in the world we live in,
what is pondering? What is care?
The sun goes and the moon comes.
The moon goes and the sun comes.
Sun and moon alternate in the birth of the light.
The cold goes and the heat comes.
The heat goes and the cold comes.
Cold and heat alternate to complete the year.
What is going away becomes smaller.
What is coming toward us expands.
Contracting and expanding act on each other.
This is what produces advantages for us.
The little inchworm curls up when it wants to expand.
Dragons and snakes hibernate
to store up and save their life-energy.
Let the essence of this thought penetrate you!
It will bring peace to your life.

It will exalt your power and virtue.

Beyond this we transcend knowing.

When you meet the spirits and understand transformation,

then your power and virtue will be complete."

One day Change said to someone:

Confined by stone. You lean on thistles.

You enter your house and do not see your consort.

The Way is closed.

(Hexagram *47 Confining*)

The Master said to him:

"Distressed by what is not distressing.

Surely your name will be disgraced if you go on like this.

You are leaning on what does not support you.

Your life is in danger.

Disgraced and endangered, your death is drawing near.

Is it any wonder that you cannot see your wife?"

One day Change said to someone:

A prince shoots a hawk on a high rampart above him.

He catches it. There is nothing that is not advantageous.

(Hexagram *40 Loosening*)

The Master said to him:

"Listen—the hawk is a bird, the bow and arrow is a weapon,

the man is a hunter. That is you.

A Realizing Person conceals the weapon within himself.

He waits, then he acts.

How can there not be success? There is nothing to hold him back.

He goes forth and takes his quarry.

The lesson for you here is: Move when your weapons are ready."

One day Change said to someone:
Locked in the stocks
Your feet disappear.
Without fault.
(Hexagram *21 Gnawing and Biting Through*)

The Master said to him:
"The Small in a person has no shame
when he is not benevolent
and no fear when he is not righteous.
When it does not see gain, it does not move.
When it is not threatened, it does not correct itself.
Correcting the Small in ourselves
is the most important rule of conduct.
This minor punishment is without fault."

One day Change said to someone:
Why are you locked in a wooden cangue so your ears disappear?
The Way is closed.
(Hexagram *21 Gnawing and Biting Through*)

The Master said to him:
"If the good does not accumulate within you,
you will have no name.
If the bad does not accumulate within you,
you will not be destroyed.
So the Small in a person says:
'A small good is nothing'
and does not do it.
It says: 'A small evil harms nothing'
and does not let go of it.
So evils accumulate until they cannot be covered over.
Guilt is so great it cannot be wiped out.

Why are you locked in a wooden cangue
so your ears disappear?
Because you will not hear Change."

One day Change said to someone:
Resting from obstruction.
For the Great Person the Way is open.
It disappears, it disappears!
Attach it to a grove of mulberry trees.
(Hexagram *12 Obstruction*)

The Master explained to him:
"Danger happens when you think you are safe.
Loss happens when you think your goods are secure.
Confusion happens when you try to control everything.
A Realizing Person does not forget danger when safe.
He does not forget loss when he is secure.
He does not forget confusion when things are in order.
His mind is always double.
This way you protect yourself
and through you the people are protected."

One day Change said to someone:
The Vessel's stand is severed.
The prince's meal is overturned.
His form is soiled. The Way is closed.
(Hexagram *50 Vessel*)

The Master said to him:
"Your power and virtue are shallow, but your office is high.
Your plans are great
but your strength is small.
Your responsibilities are heavy.

It is seldom this does not end in disaster.
Change is speaking of someone who is not equal to his task."

One day Change said to someone:
The limits turn you to stone.
Do not complete the day.
Divination: the Way is open.
(Hexagram *16 Providing for*)

The Master said to him:
"Is it not like a spirit to know the seeds?
A Realizing Person does not fawn on those above.
He is not contemptuous of those below.
This is because he knows the seeds,
the secret beginnings of Change.

Seeds move subtly. They are the beginning of opening the Way.
Using Change, the Realizing Person sees the seeds
and acts immediately.
Why should you wait until the end of the day?
The limits are turning you to stone. Why wait a whole day to act?
Through Change,
a Realizing Person knows the subtle and the obvious,
the supple and the strong.
So act with Change and be a model for the myriad people."

One day Change said to one of the pupils:
Do not keep returning at a distance.
Do not merely repent.
The Way is fundamentally open.
(Hexagram *24 Returning*)

The Master said of this:
"This son of Yan sees the limits and the seeds.
When something is wrong, he sees it.
Seeing, he does not repeat it."

One day Change said to someone:
*If three people are moving,
by consequence they will be diminished by one person.
If one person is moving,
by consequence he acquires a friend.*
(Hexagram *41 Diminishing*)

The Master said to him:
"Heaven and Earth intermingle and generate.
The myriad things transform and mature.
Male and female mix their seed.
The myriad people transform and come to life.
This speaks of the consequences of uniting with someone.
This is what is coming."

One day Change said to someone:
*This absolutely does not augment you!
Perhaps it will attack you.
You establish your heart without perseverance.
The Way is closed.*
(Hexagram *42 Augmenting*)

The Master said to him:
"Listen—this is what a Realizing Person does.
He makes himself tranquil before he moves.
He takes Change into his mind before he speaks.
He establishes a connection, then asks for something.

He cultivates these three things and is completely successful.
You, however—your movements are precarious,
so people do not join you.
Your speech is anxious, not knowing Change,
so people do not respond.
You do not establish a connection
before you implore people to help you,
so they do not join in what you do.
When no one will join you,
harm most certainly will draw near."

大
傳

Meeting your Spirit

This is a Taoist Teaching

This Teaching again shows us a Master at work, relating the answer given by Change to an individual person's life and destiny.

This section was later adopted by Confucians and said to be a description of Confucius himself, who firmly rejected divination as a spiritual practice. The overlay of Confucian terms shows this annexation, as does the attitude that these are not divinations, but general philosophical statements. Underneath, however, I can feel the Master at work, weaving the images into someone's life. However profound these comments may be, they are not just general truths. They come, I believe, from actual questions put to Change by specific people. Each example gives the person who posed the question an answer and an image or symbol that they can hold in mind, turning and rolling it in their heart to guide their action. This shows a style of divination associated with the individual use of Change as a spiritual Way. It is a mixture of teaching, prediction and warning. The Master knows the texts in detail but creates an individual meaning for each person they confront. This is not a product of laborious rational analysis. He "spontaneously brings forth" these creations.

It is notable too that he uses only texts from the "transforming" or "calling" lines. These were, evidently, of primary importance in determining the potential outcome of an action. The kind of analysis that would take over Change in the Confucian school—the hierarchical worth of line positions and the moral split between yin and yang—are nowhere to be seen.

USING CHANGE IN AN AGE OF SORROW

2.5

One day the Master said:
"Ch'ien and K'un—are they not the two-leafed gate of Change?
Ch'ien is light things. K'un is dark things.
Dark yin and light yang join their virtue
to give strong and supple lines a form.
The fates given by Heaven and Earth
take shape through these forms.
This is how we can penetrate to the bright spirits.
The Names of the figures are different,
but they cover the Ways of all things.
When we ponder the things they evoke,
we see that they are the thoughts of a time of sorrow.
Thus they can particularly help us.
Change shows us what has gone by
and interprets what is coming.
It makes the subtle seeds manifest and opens the obscure.
It distinguishes these things by means of the Names of the figures.
It completes the description
with incisive words and decisive signs.
The Names are Small (yin). What they reach to is Great (yang).
Their meanings reach far and their words have elegance.
The words twist and turn but always hit the center.
They set things forth openly,
yet always contain the wordless secret.
The two signs guide people's actions.
They show the retribution or reward that awaits."

大傳

Using Change in an Age of Sorrow

This is a Taoist Teaching

This is another very beautiful Teaching that could easily be in a Taoist book of meditations. I am convinced that we can hear a real voice that runs through much of this work, just as I am convinced that the divinations are real examples, not just moral sermons. Here the Master speaks again. His description of what Change is and does is complex and profound, but there is no trace of the Confucian moral dichotomy we have seen in previous Teachings. The two powers are the two-leaved gate of Change, dark and light, yin and yang. They give form to the series of lines in a diagram. The diagrams and what goes with them, the Names and the words are the equivalent of the way that Heaven and Earth shape the fate of each individual being. We can use these figures to penetrate the intelligence of the spirits.

The names of these figures are quite different, but, according to the Master, they cover the "Ways," the individual paths, of everything in the world we live in. If we really ponder the things that these figures bring out, if we feel the associations they call up in us, we can see they were brought together in a time of sorrow. This is another connection to the central term "Change" or I. One of the meanings of I specifically refers to unpredictable change. A sudden storm just as the crops are ripe, the disappearance of a flock of sheep, being cheated in the market, the breakdown of political order, the sudden loss of a loved one, anything that suddenly destabilizes things and turns the situation fluid is called I. A good translation of this aspect would be "trouble." The Change was composed in a I time, full of trouble and sorrow. Thus it can be of particular help to us in a later but equally I period.

It can help us by making the seeds or beginnings of things manifest and by opening what is usually obscure and closed. The figures do this, completed by the words and the divinatory signs. The words that name the figures may seem insignificant. What they reach to is great, for they connect us with the intelligence of the spirit.

The words of Change have many and far-reaching meanings, and their own inner elegance or pattern. But they do not move in a straight line. They are not "logical" and cannot be analyzed. They twist and turn, re-shaping our thoughts as we follow them. But they always hit the mark. They take us to the center. This is because the words are two-fold like the mind of the Way. They show things clearly, yet they never forget the wordless secret. They can never be fully explained. The two major signs—the Way is open and the Way is closed—are there specifically to guide our actions, to help us live our lives.

ACCUMULATING POWER AND VIRTUE *(TE)*

2.6

One day the Master said:
"Was not Change assembled in middle antiquity?
Did not those who did this have to deal with great sorrows?"
They showed us a way to accumulate power and virtue
to deal with the transformations of life.
This is their way to develop te:

10 Treading is the foundation of te.
It attains the goal harmoniously.
It uses harmonious actions.

15 Humbling is the handle of te.
It dignifies it and makes it shine.
It regulates the way you measure.

24 Returning is the root of te.
It is small and discriminates the beings.
It is the origin of self-knowing.

32 Persevering is the firmness of te.
It is diverse but not repressive.
It is the unity of te.

41 Diminishing is the cultivation of te.
At first it is difficult, then it is easy.
It keeps harm at a distance.

42 Augmenting is the enriching of te.
It is long-living and enriches without artifice.
It uses the rising of advantage from the seeds.

47 Confining marks off what is te.
It exhausts and interpenetrates things.
It holds few grudges.

48 The Well is the field of te.
It abides in its place yet shifts.
It shows you what is righteous.

57 Gently Penetrating is the regulation of te.
It weighs things and stays hidden.
It moves freely yet is always balanced.

大
傳

Accumulating Power and Virtue (Te)

This Teaching is common to all

The people who used Change as a spiritual path were very much concerned with te. This is an important word, almost as important as Tao, and almost impossible to translate. I use "power and virtue," a weak echo. The word suggests a number of concepts: power, virtue in the sense of essential content or strength, charisma, inner strength and discriminating power, moral strength and real righteousness, the ability to live in Tao, to become the Way, and also integrity and courage. It is truly a "magical" power and influences things and people without direct contact or conscious desire.

Both things and people have te. We speak of the te of Heaven or the te of a Realizing Person. The important thing is that it can be cultivated and accumulated. According to *Ta Chuan*, you accumulate and refine te by opening yourself to Change and living through its words and symbols. Over time, you accumulate enough te to become a Realized Person, a true individual connected with the "on-going process of the real."

Here, we see a meditation on te and the way it is nurtured and developed that proceeds through comments on the names of nine of the figures of Change. They were originally divided into three columns. Someone using Change on the spiritual path would know these by heart. He might meditate on the actions and qualities. When one of these figures came up as the answer to a question, he would know that his present situation offered a particularly good chance to accumulate te.

易

II

OPEN YOUR HEART TO CHANGE

2.7

Change is a book you cannot push away.
Its Way is always shifting.
Transformation and movement,
never resting,
flow through the six empty places.
Rising and falling,
never fixed,
strong and supple transform each other.
Rules cannot confine this, for it follows only Change.
It enters and leaves in rhythm.
It teaches caution coming in and going out.
It shows clearly the causes of anxiety and calamity.
It does not act like your master or guard.
It is as if your beloved parents draw near.
First follow the words and feel their meanings in your heart.
Then suddenly the Way to act arises.
If you are unwilling to do this, the Way will not open to you.

Open Your Heart to Change

This is a Taoist Teaching

This Teaching is one of the great lyric poems of Change. It describes the unceasing flow of life—moving and transforming—through the six empty places of a figure.

Nothing is ever fixed here. What happens cannot be circumscribed by rules or analysis. It is life itself, ever-changing, in its rhythmic dance of entrances and exits. The lesson Change teaches is caution, particularly at the threshold of any action. Look into the seeds. See what the results of your desires might be. But the spirit of Change is not a master or guardian. It is as if our own parents, who seek only to love, help and sustain us, draw near when we use the book. The key is allowing the words to move in your heart, and thus to move you. You cannot "figure out" what Change means. You cannot push it away through systems of thought. You must yield to the words, let them enter you and shape you from within. Then, and only then, the rules of conduct and the true Way to act in accordance with the tao will spontaneously arise. If you are unwilling to let Change into your heart, this Way will not open to you.

THE VALUE OF THE POSITIONS

2.8

Change plumbs the beginnings
and displays the ends.
That is the essential.
The six lines mix according to the moment of time.
The beginning line is difficult to understand.
The top line is easy to understand.
They are the root and the branch.
The words at the first line are tentative.
The words at the end are complete.
To explore the virtues and qualities of things,
to discriminate between what should and should not occur,
we need the middle lines.
Look! Even the most important things,
even life and death,
the opening and closing of the Way
and the flow of time can be known.
To know these things,
simply look at the Image and the words.
Immediately you have a grip on more than half of it.
The lines tell the rest.
The second and fourth line are equal in quality
but differ in position,
so their value is different.
Second lines are honored.
Fourth lines are apprehensive because of what is near.

In the Way of the supple, it is good not to be distant.
It is important to be without fault.
Its function is to be opened and centrally placed.
Third and fifth lines are equal in quality
but differ in position,
so their value is different.
For third lines the Way is often closed,
while fifth lines achieve things.
One is lowly and the other is noble.
Surely, the supple and opened is in danger here,
while the strong and whole brings success.

大
傳

The Value of the Positions

This is a Confucian Teaching

If the previous Teaching was a lyric about Change and how it cannot be confined to rules, this is its antithesis. This is the beginning of a system of analyzing the positions of the lines that would completely alter how people look at Change.

This analytic approach covers up the face of the Master who told us to "let Change into our heart" and replaces it with a system of analysis of the moral value of line positions according to the yin-yang dichotomy. It begins with numbers: even-numbered places are yin, odd-numbered places are yang. This gave rise to a system of "correspondence" between pairs of lines (when 1&4, 2&5 or 3&6 form a yin-yang pair) and the idea of "appropriateness" of a line to a place (yang lines in uneven places and yin lines in even places). Here we see its beginnings. It became an all-encompassing system that literally changed the meaning and order of the words to make their meaning fit Confucian morality. The hermeneutic battle fought out in the following years pitted the words and the spontaneous emergence of meaning in the heart against a system of interpretation that predetermines what each phrase must mean.

易

THE WAYS OF CHANGE

2.9

As a book, Change is broad, great and complete in every way.
It has the Way of Heaven in it.
It has the Way of Humanity in it.
It has the Way of Earth in it.
Change brings the Three Powers together
and doubles them to make the six places.
The six places embody nothing other
than the Way of the Three Powers.
The Way transforms and moves, so we speak of the lines.
The lines have different places,
so we speak of the things they describe.
The things are mixed together,
so we speak of the words that explain the patterns.
The words are not explicit in giving us advice
so we speak of the signs that show the Way is open or closed.

The Ways of Change

This is a Confucian Teaching

This Teaching gives us another kind of description of how Change "contains" the Way (Tao) and the potency (te) of the powers that make up the universe. These Three Powers are Heaven, Earth and Humanity between them, the "All-Under-Heaven" (T'ien Hsia). Change, we are told, participates in all of these powers. In fact, it embodies nothing other than these powers. The spirit, the shen, is left out.

Change brings the Three Powers together through its symbolizing and doubles them to get the six empty places of a gua or diagram. This gave rise to the idea that the first two lines represented Earth, the middle two represented the human world and the top two represented Heaven. Because this Way transforms and moves, there are "transforming" or "calling" lines that change into their opposite and lines that "move" without changing form. Each place, from the first at the bottom to the sixth at the top, describes certain specific things. The words attached to the lines that occupy these places explain the patterns of things. Because the words are not always clear about what we should do, there are divinatory signs attached to show us if the Way is open or closed. This is a method of analysis based entirely on line positions. It relegates the words and the spontaneity the words imply to a very secondary position. It seeks to create rules that can explain Change. This is the counter pole to the Way of the Master.

THE AGE OF CHANGE

2.10

Change was assembled and flourished
at the end of the Yin kings
and the beginning of the bountiful power and virtue
of the Chou kings.
Isn't this fitting?
It was used in the struggle between King Wen of Chou
and the tyrant Tchou. Isn't this fitting?
This is why the symbols so often warn of danger.
If, like the kings of Chou, you are aware of danger,
you can find peace and security.
If you are careless,
you will be overthrown like the tyrant Tchou.
The Way of Change is so great
it sustains everything without fail.
It instills caution about beginnings and ends
so people can live without fault.
This is the Way of Change.

The Age of Change

This is a Confucian Teaching

This Teaching has a historical base. Change, *originally called* Change of the Chou Kings (Chou I), *was first assembled around 1100 BCE, in the time when the Chou nobles were rising against their Shang overlords.*

The Oracle was used by the Chou nobles in their struggle to overthrow the last of the Shang kings, a notorious and vicious tyrant. The emergence of the Chou unified the peoples of China, and was seen as the return of a Golden Age. Thus the association is double. The Change will help you in a time of trouble, as it helped the Chou kings. And it can bring about a "Golden Age" by helping you live "without fault." The interesting thing to note is that at the time of the creation of *Ta Chuan*, the use of this powerful tool had passed from the hands of kings to private individuals.

BEING IN HARMONY
WITH CHANGE

2.11

Ch'ien is strongest in the world we live in.

Its power and virtue is the easy and spontaneous,

because it understands danger.

K'un is most supple in the world we live in.

Its power and virtue is the simple,

because it understands obstruction.

The one brings joy to our hearts, the other resolves our anxieties.

The Way of Change determines

if the Way is open or closed

in the world we live in.

Resolute and unwearied,

it completes everything in the world we live in.

Thus change and transformation speak to us:

The omens and signs tell when the Way is open.

The symbols show us what we can do.

The oracle shows us the future.

Heaven and Earth determined the places here.

The Sage-Mind brought out the potential.

Change gives us access

to the thoughts of humans

and the thoughts of the spirits.

The Eight Diagrams communicate the symbols

by making the figures.

The calling lines and the attached words

speak of the circumstances.

Strong and supple lines cluster together
so we can see if the Way is open or closed.
The transformations and the movements
speak of what is advantageous.
They shift according to the circumstances.
Thus love and hate attack each other
and the Way opens or closes.
What is far and what is near
struggle for control,
and repenting, or shame and confusion appear.
Truth and lies influence each other,
and advantage or injury appears.
All these relations are in Change.
When things that are related to each other by nature
cannot find harmony, the Way closes.
This brings injury, repenting, or shame and confusion.

One day the Master said:
"You must listen to a person's words.
When someone is planning subversion,
his words are clothed in shame.
The words of a person with doubt in his heart go on and on.
A person for whom the Way is open uses few words.
An agitated person uses many words.
A slanderous person uses vacillating words.
A person who has lost his integrity uses twisted words.
Which of these people hears Change?"

大傳

Being in Harmony with Change

This is a Taoist Teaching

The two greatest powers in the world are available to us through Change. Ch'ien is strong and easy. Because it understands danger and how to deal with it, it brings joy to our hearts. K'un is supple and simple. Because it understands obstructions and how to deal with them, it resolves all our anxieties. This is the gift of Change. It shows us if the Way is open or closed and tells us how any action will come to completion. It speaks directly through its omens, its symbols and the fact that we can consult it as an oracle.

Change is not a human invention, though humans obviously assembled it. It reflects something greater. Heaven and Earth gave it the six places. The Sage-Mind brought out the potential through symbols and words. Change acts as a key. It opens things. By taking it to heart, it gives us

access to the thoughts of humans and the bright spirits. Everything has a function in this "mediumistic" gift. The Eight Diagrams come together to form the Figures. The Figures bring out the hidden symbols. The calling lines and attached words tell us what our circumstances really are. Strong and supple lines cluster in a particular way to let us see if the Way is open or closed. The calling lines and the lines that move without changing tell us what is advantageous for us to do. Everything shifts according to the time, the circumstances, and the movement of the spirits.

Change lets us see the great forces in the world as they grapple with each other: love and hate, hot desire and cool thought, truth and lies. The Way opens and it closes. The worst, however, is when things that belong together cannot find harmony.

But you must be willing to listen. Change shows the Way, but not everyone can hear it. Your heart must be open and pure. The Master said that we can tell much by listening to people's words. Change is always there, ready to speak. Are you willing to hear its answers?

易

Index

Acknowledgements

Carroll and Brown Limited would like to thank

Production
Karol Davies
Clair Reynolds

IT Management
Elisa Merino
Paul Stradling

Picture Research
Carrie Haines
Richard Soar

Index
Madeline Weston

Photography
Photographs by David Murray pp. 61, 71, 80,
83, 91, 99, 101, 105, 128-129, 133, 139, 143, 145, 153

AKG p. 31; Bridgeman pp. 11, 15, 28, 42;
Robert Harding pp. 12, 34, 51; Images pp. 20, 49;
Tony Stone pp. 65, 119, 150